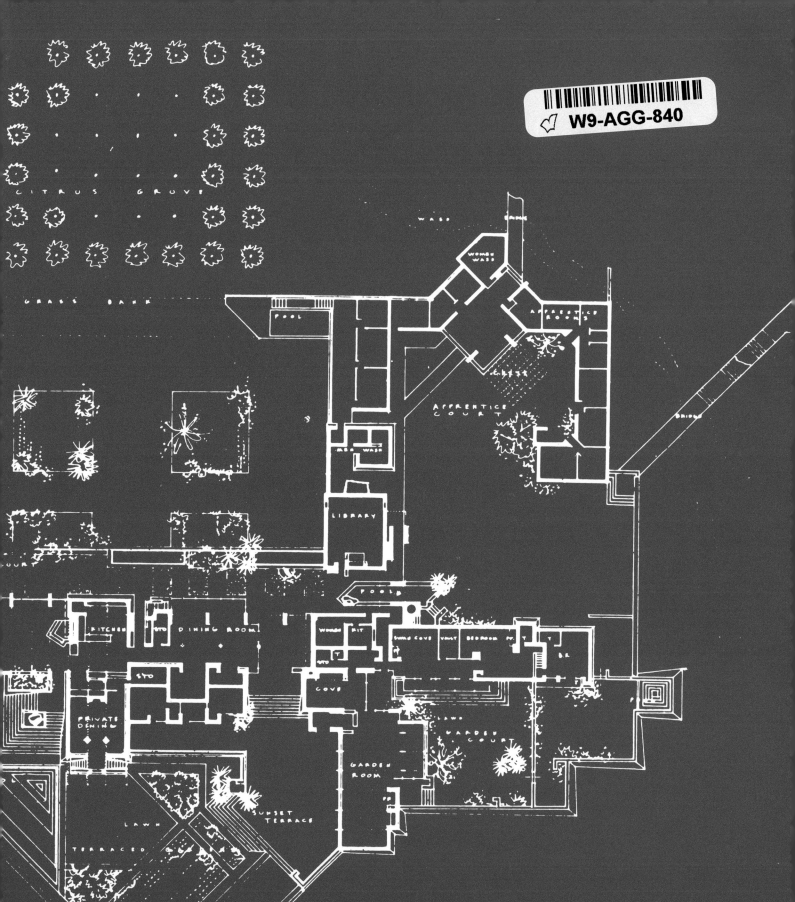

ARCHITECTS HOUSE THEMSELVES: BREAKING NEW GROUND

ARCHITECTS HOUSE THEMSELVES:
BREAKING NEW GROUND

Michael Webb

Foreword by J. Carter Brown

THE PRESERVATION PRESS
NATIONAL TRUST FOR HISTORIC PRESERVATION

The Preservation Press
National Trust for Historic Preservation
1785 Massachusetts Avenue, N.W.
Washington, D.C. 20036

Printed in Hong Kong by Palace Press International

10 9 8 7 6 5 4 3 2 1 98 97 96 95 94
Library of Congress Cataloging-in-Publication Data

Webb, Michael, 1937–
Architects House Themselves: Breaking New Ground / Michael Webb.
p. cm.
Includes bibiographical references.
ISBN 0-89133-241-3
1. Architect-designed houses—United States. 2.Architecture, Modern—20th century—United States, I. Title.
NA7208.W4   1994   93-32477
728'.092'273—dc20

Book and cover designed by Arnold and Isolde Schwartzman
Cover design in homage to Charles and Ray Eames's House of Cards, photographed by Garry Brod
Endpapers: Plan of *Taliesin West*, Scottsdale, Arizona (© Frank Lloyd Wright Foundation)
Frontispiece: Stair hall of Herbert and Edna Newman's house in Woodbridge, Connecticut
(© 1984 Norman McGrath)

ACKNOWLEDGMENTS

MY THANKS GO TO Buckley Jeppson, director of The Preservation Press, for his faith in this project, and to Deborah Styles and Janet Walker for their skill in guiding the book to publication. It was made possible and pleasurable to write by the generous cooperation of more than 150 architects, who offered their houses for consideration or recommended others. A lack of space prevented me from including all the good work I saw.

For information on the classic houses, I would like to thank Robert L. Sweeney, president of the Friends of the Schindler House; the College of Environmental Design at California State Polytechnic University, Pomona, custodians of the Neutra house; Arnold Roy and the staff at Taliesin West for a warm welcome. Also to Nancy Curtis, Lorna Condon, and Peter Gittleman of the Society for the Preservation of New England Antiquities, which maintains the Gropius house so well; and to Eames Demetrios and Shelley Mills, who have given the Eames house a new lease on life.

J. Carter Brown, a patron and afficionado of architecture, generously contributed the foreword. Thomas S. Hines reviewed the opening chapters and made several valuable suggestions. Elizabeth McMillian, Elizabeth Sverbeyeff Byron, Pilar Viladas, Julia Bloomfield, Anne W. Lowe, Carter H. Manny, Jr., Steven Dumas, and Cameron McNall provided introductions and recommendations. Mary Jane O'Donnell, Peggy Loar, Hugh and Tiziana Hardy, Joel and Janet Levinson, James Marlas, and Patrick Macrory revived my spirits with their hospitality. My greatest debt is to the architects and photographers credited on the pages that follow.

■   ■   ■

Houses are dated from the beginning of the design process through completion. Most of the remarks by living architects are taken from interviews with the author; other quotations are from books and articles cited under Further Reading. The houses by Schindler, Neutra, Wright, and Gropius are open to the public. Please respect the privacy of the other residents.

MICHAEL WEBB

CONTENTS

SHELTER. HOME. What in our lives is at once more necessary and more intimate than the place in which we live? Michael Webb's brilliant book is, as well, both intimate and necessary. We are all born voyeurs. What a treat to be able to peek inside the creations and creativity of so many gifted architects. At the same time, the underlying thesis is a needful one. Here is a handbook and a catalyst to shake us loose from a passive and unexamined acceptance of the trite.

Many architects I have known have been too fearful to design their own houses. They are trained professionally to respond to the needs and—yes—the whims of others; the self-searching and exposure that architects' own houses necessitate threaten to expose and fuse their public and private personae. Paul Rudolph points out that without an outside client, a designer has "no sounding board." Any architect would tell you that when he has the right client, the constraints often unleash fresh creativity.

Yet many architects have taken on the challenge of being their own clients with superb results, as this book attests. Many have used the opportunity for experimentation, testing both artistic innovations and new materials and technologies. Among the six classics that begin this book (each one, as it happens, in my personal pantheon of great architectural experiences), Neutra's own VDL Research House has a particular significance for this writer. Recently commissioned to read a paper in a symposium sponsored by UCLA and the Getty Trust in conjunction with the Neutra centennial, I came across my father's correspondence praising that house in 1937. This was on a visit made in the course of Neutra's designing, with an extraordinary amount of input from the couple who were his clients, the summer house, "Windshield," in which I grew up. (It has, sadly, not been preserved, having been annihilated by a fire after the house was no longer ours.)

Neutra in that case was not designing for himself, but for a patron who was a student of architectural history, with a drawing board and T-square in his study all his life. John Nicholas Brown was determined to help move the art of architecture ahead, and specifically indicated to Neutra his desire for a contrast to the colonial family house in Providence, now a center for study in his memory. No one was, at the same time, more supportive than my father of historic preservation; and it is greatly to the credit of the National Trust for Historic Preservation that it should have undertaken to publish this book.

For, like Janus, we must look both backward and ahead. Michael Webb's book does just that. His personal experience of the varied exemplars he describes, his deft characterizations and pungent quotes, and his belief in the relevance of daring make this Janus-like study a landmark in its own right. ∎

J. CARTER BROWN
Chairman, U.S. Commission of Fine Arts
Director Emeritus, National Gallery of Art

WHAT SETS ARCHITECTS' own houses apart from those of their neighbors? Training, personal convictions, and the challenge of showing what they can do for themselves and others impel them to take risks and try something out of the ordinary. Tight budgets, the petty tyranny of neighborhood design review boards, and the knowledge that they will have to live in what they have built (or remodeled) discipline their fantasies. Out of that mix of freedom and constraints come the adventurous solutions explored in this book.

All but the most radical architects look to the past and to the site for inspiration. Thomas Jefferson pointed the way, fusing European tradition and American invention at Monticello, a house he enjoyed "putting up and pulling down" over four decades. Lewis Mumford called it "a prototype of the apartment and the bungalow."

If Jefferson were reborn, the revolutionary in him might enjoy all six of the classic modern houses that launch this survey. Now that they have achieved landmark status, it is easy to forget that each was, like Monticello, a laboratory for new ideas, enlarging our concept of "house." Built between 1921 and 1949, these houses showed how elastic modernism could be.

Rudolph Schindler and Richard Neutra were lured from Vienna to America by their admiration for Frank Lloyd Wright and settled in Los Angeles.

Schindler built a desert camp of concrete, wood, and canvas, with outdoor living rooms and rooftop sleeping porches. Neutra created a silvery, transparent stack of flowing rooms and decks for the contemplation of nature; a machine in the garden. Walter Gropius combined Bauhaus rationality and the New England vernacular in his family house near Boston.

Frank Lloyd Wright headed west from Wisconsin with the dedication of a pioneer and spent two decades building and refining a compound that hugged the Arizona desert in a tight embrace. Charles and Ray Eames ordered a steel frame for a single-story house that was to extend from a hillside to overlook the Pacific, then used the same parts to enclose a two-story house and studio against the hill. Philip Johnson built, on a Connecticut meadow, a steel and glass pavilion that subtly adapted the rigorous geometry of Mies van der Rohe.

All six houses have become icons that inspire fresh ways of containing and inflecting space, of encompassing a way of life and relating buildings to the land. Their idealism is contagious, their capacity to surprise undiminished.

Forty recent houses and apartments from across the United States and one from Canada have been chosen for their innovative qualities and incidentally for their diversity of size, purpose, character, and location. I have shown a preference for jobs that do a lot with a little, stretching tight sites and budgets as far as they will go. That may explain the preponderance of examples from southern California, long a magnet for free spirits and fresh ideas.

Here, grouped loosely by theme, are inventive remodelings and houses that rework traditional forms; houses tailored to the needs of a solitary poet from Costa Rica and an extended family from Taiwan; daring experiments and houses that cling to "unbuildable" sites; high-rise apartments and weekend retreats. The thematic groupings show how different architects tackle similar issues, but most of these houses could be listed under several headings.

What do they have in common? Architects tend to be poorer than their clients, so they test their ingenuity by shoehorning houses into steep or narrow plots, reaching upward—even on rustic sites—to achieve privacy and views. The most irregular buildings have a strong axiality or modular rhythm to articulate the spatial complexity, recalling the description of architecture as "frozen music." Ceiling heights shift dramatically, and boundaries between rooms and the outdoors are blurred. Like flowers turning toward the sun, windows (undraped) are often placed eccentrically to frame views rather than to create a symmetrical pattern on the facade. Window walls defy climatic extremes, serving as solar collectors in winter and depending on trees or projecting roof planes for shade in summer.

Architects often have unconventional priorities. They will expose industrial grade materials to demonstrate their ability to save money but spend freely on hand-crafted joints and furnishings. They have a fondness for lofty, white, or woodsy all-purpose rooms, often accented with splashes of emphatic color, and bedrooms that shrink to closet size—as at Monticello. Narrow, unrailed stairs lead to "storage areas" that serve every purpose but. Chairs tend to be few and uncomfortable, but exquisitely crafted or engineered. Nolli's 12-sheet map of Rome in 1750, building models, and folk art are favorite collectibles; these, like the chairs, are usually well spaced, but Charles Moore has made it respectable to turn your house into a cabinet of curiosities. The more affluent or well-connected display serious modern art.

This inventory, like the thematic groupings, suggests affinities but misses the essential point: that each house is one of a kind, a reflection of circumstances and the personality of its designer(s). You may find one or several you would love to move into, or you may begin checking off things you like and loathe about each. As you do, reflect on how little choice builders offer you. Consider how suburban developments squander land yet offer buyers views of little but asphalt and a neighbor's wall. Look again at that fiberglass portico and marble trim: do they enhance the house or merely convey an aura of status? Does a new house have to be as standardized and predictable as a Detroit sedan?

Driving around America, I am alternately exhilarated by its regional diversity and depressed by the way it is being homogenized. From coast to coast, on mountain, plain, and shore, one finds the same spec-built houses clustered in identical Olde Townes and Quail Runs; crude pastiches of a generic past that ignore the local vernacular and obliterate the topography. Is this what Americans dream of, or—lacking affordable alternatives—settle for? Surely they deserve better?

Many architects see their own houses as prototypes but are frustrated in their efforts to apply their ideas in the marketplace by the innate conservatism of planning authorities, developers, and a public that has been conditioned to demand a traditional product. Those with the means to please themselves are deterred by loan officers, appraisers, and well-meaning friends, who insist that they'll never be able to sell a house that differs from the norm. There is nothing surprising about this: resistance to the unfamiliar is a basic human trait. Sadly, it cuts us off from experiences that could enrich our lives. The developers' mantra, "traditional: warm and cozy; modern: cold and unfriendly," sounds like an echo of the

pigs in *Animal Farm*. There is good and bad in both, and the possibilities for mixing the best of each are unlimited.

In 1938, the Oscar-winning actress Luise Rainer wrote to Richard Neutra about her apartment in west Los Angeles, which he had newly completed. She explained that she had long hesitated to live in a modern house, convinced that "one could never feel warm or at home. How different it is...the moment you live inside!" she continued. "The clearness, the long lines of windows which allow the light to come in and the eye to rove out far, far, all this gives you a strange feeling of happiness and freedom."

For much of the 1940s, Charles and Ray Eames lived in that apartment; it helped inspire their work and the house they would build for themselves. Over the past 16 years, I've had the good fortune to live there myself. The shock of the new has long since worn off, the silver-framed white cubes have been enveloped by trees in the hillside courtyard, the cool volumes of adjoining apartments comfortably house students, a retired couple, families, other bachelors, traditional furnishings, and the minimalism I prefer. They have won a historic landmark designation, and they continue to demonstrate the rewards of taking risks, the adventure of breaking new ground. ■

West Hollywood, California, 1921–22

"THE ORDINARY residential arrangement providing rooms for specialized purposes has been abandoned. Instead, each person receives a large private studio; each couple, a common entrance hall and bath. Open porches on the roof are used for sleeping. An enclosed patio for each couple, with an out-of-door fireplace, serves the purposes of an ordinary living room. The form of the house divides the garden into several such private rooms. A separate guest apartment, with its own garden, is also provided for. One kitchen is planned for both couples. The wives take alternate weekly responsibility for dinner menus, and so gain periods of respite from the incessant household rhythm."

Thus did Rudolph Schindler describe his "cooperative dwelling for two young couples," the idealistic commune that launched his architectural practice in Los Angeles and remained his home-studio until his death. He had studied architecture under Otto Wagner in Vienna, moved to Chicago in 1914, and was sent to Los Angeles by Frank Lloyd Wright to supervise construction of the Hollyhock House while the Master struggled to complete the Imperial Hotel in Tokyo. He was the first of several immigrants to plant the seeds of European modernism in southern California, where they bloomed and mutated a decade before the Bauhaus refugees fertilized New England.

In 1921 Schindler bought a 100 x 200-foot plot on undeveloped King's Road, a

block from the now-demolished Dodge House, which Irving Gill had built five years earlier. Inspired by a camping trip in Yosemite National Park, he designed a 3,450-square-foot, pinwheel plan house that was part cave, part tent. As he explained, "each room has a concrete wall for back, and a garden front with a

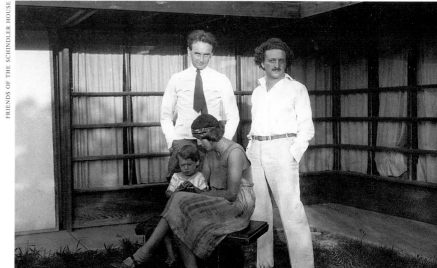

FRIENDS OF THE SCHINDLER HOUSE

Rudolph Schindler (right), with Richard and Dione Neutra and their son Dion in 1928.

large opening fitted with sliding doors. This opening is protected by an overhanging roof, carried by two cantilever beams crossing the rooms. These beams serve at the same time as supports for sliding light fixtures, and for movable partitions. The shape of the rooms, their relation to the patios and the alternating roof levels, create an entirely new spatial interlock between the interior and the garden."

Schindler intended that the house be "a simple weave of a few structural

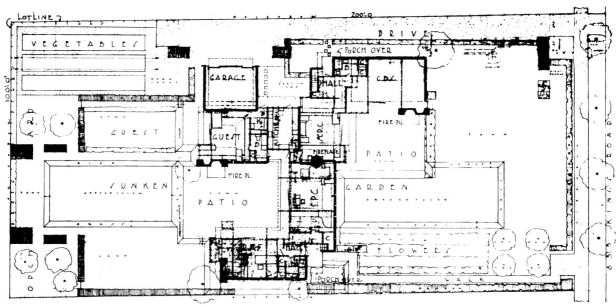

RESIDENCE·R·M·S·HOLLYWOOD·CALIFORNIA·

materials which retain their natural color and texture throughout." Like a Japanese tea house, its roughness contains a world of meaning. There is a strong Japanese influence (filtered through the Vienna Secession and Wright) in the insistent horizontality of the window walls and redwood eaves and in the removable canvas sliding screens. Balancing the lightness of wood and canvas are the walls of tilt-up concrete slabs, separated by slots of glass, which suggest an industrial version of the adobe walls Schindler had admired on a trip through New Mexico.

California cast its spell on him, as on so many other newcomers, distracting him from the reality of chilly nights and winter rains. The open sleeping porches had to be enclosed with glass. There was no mechanical heating, though each room

had a fireplace, and no communal room except the tiny kitchen, which the wives sometimes declined to share. The first young couple, Clyde and Marion Chace, left for Florida after three years. Richard Neutra, a friend from Vienna, and his wife, Dione, took their place, but Dione's cello practicing drove Pauline Schindler to distraction, and she later decamped. Schindler's architectural partnership with Neutra foundered, but he stayed on, and Pauline returned, living in one half of the house and passing notes to her estranged husband in the other. She continued to host the liveliest, most progressive salon in the city.

Right: One of the patio entrances to the house as it looked in the 1950s.

Overleaf: Restored interior with its vertical slits and clerestory windows. (© JULIUS SHULMAN)

The roof during the final stage of restoration, showing the open sleeping porches .

When Pauline Schindler died, in 1977, the property was rescued from predatory developers and restored to its original purity by the non-profit Friends of the Schindler House. Their president, Robert L. Sweeney, and consulting architect, Peter J. Snell, stripped additions, replaced rotting timbers, and created reproductions to supplement what had survived of Schindler's original furniture. Equally important was the recreation of the outdoor living areas, enclosed by hedge walls, which extend out from the house on three sides. Schindler saw California as a terrestrial paradise and made an ally of nature.

A minimal shelter, crudely made, the house has had to struggle for recognition as a landmark of modernism. Its influence on other architects, especially in Los Angeles, has never been greater than today. Complex and contradictory, it is rugged and delicate, open and enclosed, intricate and free-flowing, rough and sensual. It is a house made by hand, full of promise and passion; a sketch that Schindler and others would flesh out in decades to come. ■

VDL Research House, Los Angeles, 1932–39; rebuilt 1964–66 with Dion Neutra (1926–)

RICHARD NEUTRA followed Schindler from Vienna to Los Angeles by way of Zurich —where he met his future wife, Dione Niedermann. Along the way he found work in Chicago and with Wright in Wisconsin. Later he wrote, "In Southern California, I found what I had hoped for, a people who were more 'mentally foot-loose' than those elsewhere; who did not mind deviating opinions...where one can do almost anything that comes to mind...."

It was an optimistic assessment. Neutra was sustained more by faith than by commissions during his first decade of practice, which began with Schindler in 1925. They collaborated on a competition entry for the League of Nations building, but the partnership broke up after Neutra secured the commission from Dr. Philip Lovell, a former Schindler client, to design his ambitious steel-framed Health House (1927–29) in the Hollywood Hills.

That icon of modernism, with its gleaming white planes leaping into space, launched Neutra's reputation and lured a Dutch industrialist, Cornelius Van der Leeuw, to Los Angeles. A patron of mod-ern architecture, he was shocked to learn

Richard Neutra beside the rooftop solarium and reflecting pool in the late 1960s.

that Neutra lived in a rented bungalow, and loaned him $3,000 to help him build a new house. In gratitude, the architect called it the VDL Research House, though he had to borrow more than twice as much to finish the job.

Neutra made an inspired choice of site, a 60 x 70-foot plot facing west over the picturesque Silverlake reservoir, northwest of downtown Los Angeles, with a vista of mountains beyond. He built a taut-skinned, two-story block up to the limits of the site at the front and sides, leaving space behind for a patio. The entrance level contained a drafting room with two small apartments for apprentices. The family's living areas on the second floor led out through folding doors to an unglazed sleeping porch, from where a ladder led up to the rooftop solarium and terrace. The house was built in 1932–33; in 1939 Neutra added a one-story guest wing and playroom for his three sons, connected to service rooms

below the house and defining a patio.

Harwell Harris, an unpaid assistant to Neutra around 1930, recalled that his mentor admired in equal measure Wright's artistry and Henry Ford's mastery of standardization and mass production: "He talked of every building he designed as though it were factory-built or at least the prototype of one." Occasionally, as in the Health House, Neutra had the budget to build in steel; more often (as in his own house) he used the same stucco-clad, wood-frame technique that every California builder employed. Neutra told Harris that he painted wood frames silver "to get people accustomed to the look of the future."

The VDL house was conceived as a laboratory for materials and human responses to living in a tightly planned area of 2,100 square feet. Concrete floor joists were combined with the wood frame to permit wide window openings without incurring the expense of structural

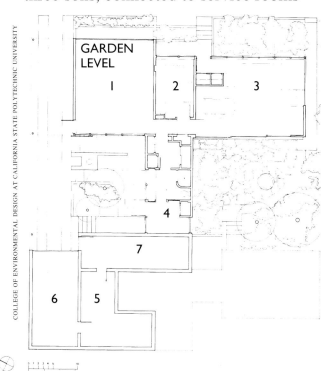

GARDEN LEVEL

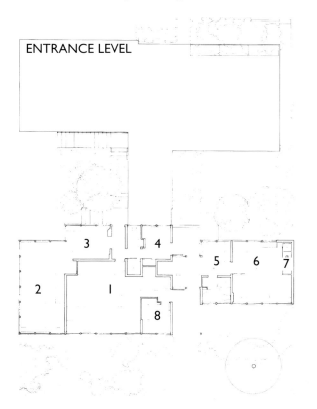

ENTRANCE LEVEL

Silverlake facade of rebuilt house with the vertical louvers that provide shade from the late afternoon sun.

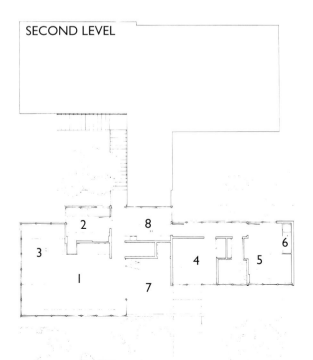

SECOND LEVEL

Plans of original house.

GARDEN LEVEL
1. Playroom 2. Kitchen 3. Garden Room
4. Guest Room 5. Utility Room 6. Garage 7. Laundry

ENTRANCE LEVEL
1. Drafting Room 2. Studio Apartment 3. Kitchen
4. Maid's Room 5. Entry 6. Office/Bedroom
7. Lift 8. Reception

SECOND LEVEL
1. Living Room 2. Kitchen 3. Dining Area
4. Bedroom 5. Bedroom 6. Lift 7. Sleeping Terrace
8. Breakfast Room

steel. Projecting roof planes shade the windows and contain recessed light channels that illuminate the garden at night, thus preserving the link between indoors and out. Neutra persuaded manufacturers to provide him with free samples of innovative building materials—enameled metal panels, cork flooring, and pressed fiber boards—so that he could test and publicize their viability. Mirror glass and extensive glazing make rooms feel larger; beds, sofas, and cabinets were built in. A monochromatic palette fostered a feeling of serenity.

The purist aesthetic, unsoftened by the trees that soon screened it from the street, shocked traditionalists. Regula Fybel, Neutra's sister-in-law, lived in the house when it was new and remembers the day that a rock was hurled through a window. Attached was an angry scrawl: "Pie Factory!"

The house was gutted by fire in 1963, but it was rebuilt on the same footprint and to a similar plan, under the supervision of Neutra's second son, Dion. Two-story automated vertical louvers and gold-tinted glass shaded windows to the west and south until the trees grew up. The penthouse was glazed and surrounded by a shallow reflecting pool to compensate for the retreat of the reservoir, which had been reconfigured and was now 600 feet away from the house. The kitchen was enlarged; windows were sealed against pollution; a music and

a seminar room replaced the old drafting studio and one of the apprentice's apartments.

When Dione Neutra died in 1990, the house was taken over as a study center by California State Polytechnic University, Pomona. Its College of Environmental Design is preparing plans and seeking funds for a badly needed restoration. Though it has been poorly maintained and the property is choked with vegetation, the house preserves the brittle elegance of its original design. From the glass entry door you look straight through to the sunken patio and the apartment on the far side. Within, space flows almost unimpededly through and out, penetrating the thinnest of membranes, with sliding windows to allow good cross ventilation. Rooms are transparent and reflective, suspended beween trees and water. The VDL House embodies Neutra's vision of a machine set in a garden, preserving the sharp distinction between the two that Schindler's blurs. ∎

Transparent and reflective living room of rebuilt house, furnished with pieces Neutra had designed in the 1930s.

Lincoln, Massachusetts, 1937–38

NEWLY ARRIVED in America to rejuvenate the Harvard School of Design, Walter Gropius studied the local vernacular and built a Bauhaus version of a colonial family home. It was his first building in the New World, and he wanted it to demonstrate the fusion of craft and industry that he had promoted as founding director of the Bauhaus, and even earlier as a pioneer of rational architecture in Berlin. There is a smooth transition from the flat-roofed, white-stucco houses he had designed with Marcel Breuer in Dessau a decade before, to the local tradition of white-painted siding, gray-painted brick chimney, screen porch, and fieldstone base. Roof deck, ribbon windows, and steel pipe columns are carried over from Europe, but the roof slopes inward to drain through a pipe protected from ice and snow.

Gropius had an idyllic four-acre site near Walden Pond, and a limited budget,

Walter Gropius in the 1940s.

both provided as a loan by Mrs. James Storrow, a philanthropic landowner who believed it was her duty to help a brilliant immigrant show what he could do. As a city dweller who idealized nature, a rationalist who prized convenience, and a devoted husband and father, Gropius planned a house that would be practical and poetic. He set it atop a small hill surrounded by an apple orchard, and he framed views with windows that are narrow on the north and east sides, expansive but shaded by trees and overhangs to the south and west. An angled entrance canopy, a projecting porch, and two white screens extend the box into the landscape.

Schindler built as though California's climate was always benign; Gropius was awed by what his wife, Ise, later described as [some of] "the most extreme and trying climatic conditions anywhere in the world." He borrowed from local tradition in putting the back door in line with the front to stimulate cross ventilation and made sure that windows could be opened all around to catch every summer breeze and to vent stale air. The big windows absorb heat from the low winter sun to supplement or to supplant the efficient hot-air and hot-water heating. The parents liked sleeping with open windows, so the master bedroom is separated from the bath and dressing area by a picture window that provides a visual link between them and conserves heat in the rest of the house.

Ise Gropius on the roof deck in 1948. Lyonel Feininger, a fellow refugee from the Bauhaus, painted the wall pink.

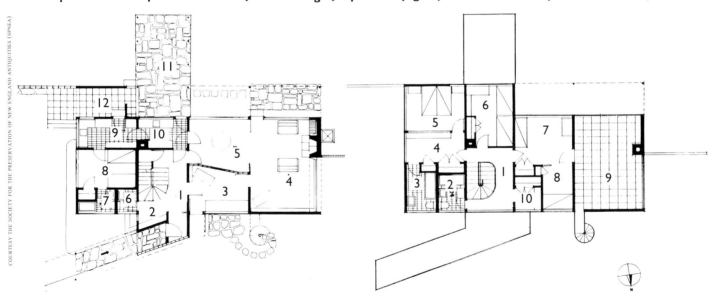

FIRST FLOOR
1. Entrance Hall 2. Coats 3. Study 4. Living Room
5. Dining Room 6. Toilet 7. Maid's Bath
8. Maid's Room 9. Kitchen 10. Pantry
11. Screened Porch 12. Service Porch

SECOND FLOOR
1. Hall 2. Bath 3. Bath 4. Dressing Room
5. Master Bedroom 6. Guest Room
7. Child's Room 8. Bed Alcove 9. Roof Deck
10. Sewing Room

Gropius adapted the traditional colonial plan of rooms opening off a central hall and stair, replacing inner walls with curtains and folding screens to achieve an easy flow of space. Working within an envelope of only 2,300 square feet on two floors, he packed in an extraordinary variety of seemingly spacious rooms, including maid's quarters, a study, and a sewing room. The Gropius's daughter Ati was 12 when the family moved in, and she wanted a place of her own. Gropius designed the second-floor deck in close proximity to her room, and installed an iron spiral stair that allowed her to take friends directly up without having first to introduce them downstairs. In her old age, Ise praised the house as "compact and frugal," qualities she said that were born of principle and of the hardships of post-war Berlin and translated well to the land of the Puritans.

Like Neutra, Gropius was dazzled by the potential of American technology and the resources of builders' catalogs. His house was a laboratory for the innovative use of industrial materials and fittings, from the open coat rack and glass brick screen in the entrance hall to the lab counters in the dressing room and the theater light sconces on the walls. Cork floors and sprayed-on acoustic plaster muffle sound. The only major feature that was not ordered from a catalog is the sinuous, hand-welded steel stair rail that ties together the two floors.

The house was conceived as a monochromatic canvas of white and gray (Bauhaus favorites) that nature would paint. Its sharp lines and thoughtfully composed vistas enhance the experience of the countryside and the changing seasons. The house also provides a backdrop for the original Bauhaus art works and the furniture, much of which was designed by Marcel Breuer, a close friend and one-time partner. The Nazis despised modern design and had closed the Bauhaus, but a Berlin professor persuaded Goebbels to authorize the release of Gropius's family effects in order to boost German prestige and, as Ise slyly recalled, to counter the French Beaux Arts influence in the United States! The furniture was put to heavy use. As the original pieces wore out, they were discarded and replaced by the latest designs.

Before Ise died in 1983, she donated the house and its contents to the Society for the Preservation of New England Antiquities (SPNEA), which has done an exemplary job of conservation and opens the house to the public every summer. Ati, who now teaches a Bauhaus-inspired course in Brooklyn, checked to see that everything was as her father left it, down to his glasses on the double desk that Breuer had designed for her parents in 1925. Conservator Peter Gittleman remarks that it was the most challenging but also the most accurate restoration that the SPNEA had ever undertaken. ∎

MICHAEL WEBB

Above: Living room in 1948 with original furniture brought from Germany.

Left: Staircase with hand-welded steel handrail linking the two floors.

Below: Entrance front. Gropius fused European modernism and the New England vernacular.

FRANK LLOYD WRIGHT (1867–1959)

Taliesin West, Scottsdale, Arizona, 1939–59

ONLY THE SUN tells you that Scottsdale is in the desert. Tasteful colonial homes and manicured lawns, shopping centers and golf courses have obliterated the sagebrush, though the odd saguaro serves as a scenic prop and an authentic, unimproved crag can be admired from the cross-town freeway. Taliesin West, the winter retreat that Frank Lloyd Wright began building here in the late 1930s, is approached through a subdivision.

"Taliesin West is a look over the rim of the world...magnificent—beyond words to describe," wrote Wright in his autobiography. Beyond the suburban sprawl, the power lines, and the smog, nature reasserts itself, and the prairie-born architect has subordinated his forms to the rocks and mountains. Low walls of boulders set in mortar support angular wood frames, painted dark red, and translucent acrylic roofs (replacing the original canvas). Like Schindler, Wright was inspired by a camping trip: a temporary cluster of canvas-topped cabins he designed in 1929 to house his family and staff while he planned a millionaires' resort near Phoenix. The stock market crash soon killed that project, but Wright never lost his love for America's last frontier. Prosaically, he went to Arizona on doctor's orders and to save on heating bills in Wisconsin; but, unlike so many newcomers, he shed his cultural baggage and took his cue from the land.

Three axes flow out of the entrance court, northeast, east, and southeast, defining two sides of an incomplete diamond of ground-hugging buildings, walkways, and gardens. Head east, beneath a pergola, past the drafting office and dining room to a kind of rock cleft at the base of a massive tower. Enter, take four quick turns, and you arrive at the threshold of Wright's living room: an experience as rewarding as that of riding down the ravine of Petra to discover the temple facade hewn from a cliff.

Wright was a master in leading people through space. The approach along this processional way, through the fissure, and into the soaring vault calls for costumed priests beating gongs. The room itself and the spaces leading out of it need no ceremony to lift the spirits. Steel-reinforced wood beams spring from the low west wall and tilt down over a glass porch that projects into a courtyard to the side of a massive stone hearth. Within this simple wedge is a dynamic alternation of high and low, bright and dark, open and enclosed. The structural module establishes a rhythm that plays out in the small projecting squares along the eaves, which

Wright in the living room in the 1950s.

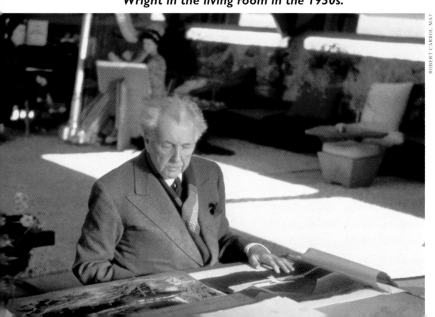

ROBERT CARROL MAY

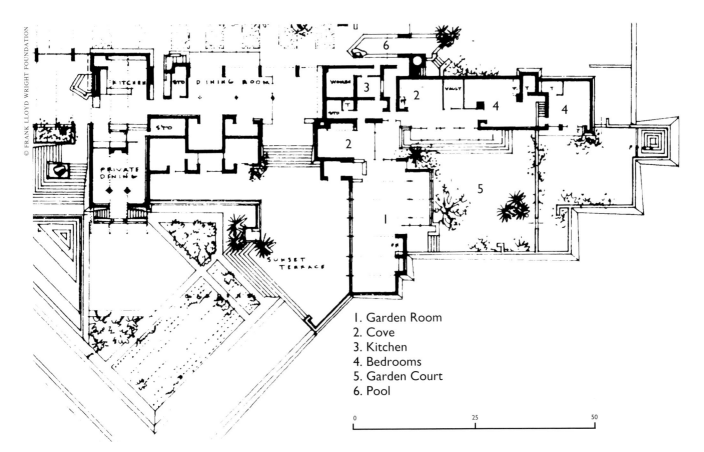

1. Garden Room
2. Cove
3. Kitchen
4. Bedrooms
5. Garden Court
6. Pool

0   25   50

cast broken shadow lines—a feature that Wright felt was characteristic of the desert. Beneath the translucent, canvas-lined ceiling is a clerestory that admits the first and last rays and the low sun of winter, but excludes summer's glare. The red painted concrete floor and wood beams absorb the desert light, giving this room the cool serenity of a tent.

Taliesin West provided Wright with an architectural laboratory. He tinkered with the living room for twenty years, adding and subtracting space, moving walls, eliminating a stair. In the 1950s he inserted the hearth, a second entrance and skylit hall, and a wood flap that dips over the south window—reputedly to screen out power lines. Outside, he extended garden walls and enclosed patios. The living room has been restored and refurnished to look as it did before Olgivanna, Wright's last wife, put her gaudy stamp on the house. But the corner kitchen and the dining room tucked in beside a second huge hearth are no more. The suite of bedrooms that extend to the east has now been converted to offices. A major accomplishment of Arnold Roy, the architect in charge of restoration, was to dismantle the roof, replace fiberglass with acrylic, and finally achieve, after 50 years, a waterproof seal.

Wood beams spring from the low west wall and support a translucent acrylic roof.

East facade and porch from courtyard. Trees and the projecting roof screen the summer sun.

Wright tinkered with the living room for 20 years, moving walls, adding a hearth, and removing a staircase.

Play of angles along the east side of the living room.

Wright called this living space the garden room—for its tree-filled courtyard, landscaped terrace and pool, and nature's cactus garden to the south. The duality is expressed on the facades: a canopied expanse of glass to the courtyard, an impervious wall and roof where the sun achieves its full power. In Wright's day, a caravan would set out from Wisconsin in fall and return in spring. Back then nobody summered in the desert. Now Taliesin West is open year round. Air-conditioning tames the Arizona furnace, but you can easily recapture the thrill of camping out beneath the stars. ∎

Pacific Palisades, California, 1945–49

IN 1945 EVERYONE anticipated an explosive demand, pent up by the Depression and the war, for improved housing. John Entenza, the crusading editor of *Arts+Architecture*, declared that it was time to stop dreaming and start building. The magazine announced it would be the client for a series of architect-designed "Case Study" houses, to be built and furnished using "war-born techniques and materials best suited to the expression of man's life in the modern world." In the December 1945 issue, Charles and Ray Eames, in collaboration with Eero Saarinen, proposed a house for themselves and one for Entenza, facing each other across a meadow, on a bluff overlooking the Pacific.

The Eameses had been living in a Neutra apartment since they arrived in Los Angeles from Cranbrook in 1941. In their proposal for "a married couple, both occupied professionally with mechanical experiment and graphic presentation," they described themselves as "basically apartment dwellers" and stipulated, "The house must make no insistent demands for itself, but rather aid as background for life in work" with nature as a "shock-absorber." Entenza wanted houses "capable of duplication." The Eameses countered with a rational design tailored to personal needs.

Their first sketch showed a single-story, steel-framed box, more apartment than house, cantilevered from the hillside and two slender metal columns, floating above the meadow. It was designed to contrast with the low, ground-hugging Entenza house. Postwar shortages delayed construction, but in late 1948, after the steel had been delivered to the site, Charles changed the design. He may have seen other, similar plans by Mies and Saarinen and decided that he could be more original and enclose much more space with the same amount of steel. Acting on his conviction that "design depends largely on constraints and the designer's enthusiasm for working within them," he sketched a two-story house and separate studio, using the same structural elements (plus one extra beam) and filling in the frame with windows, doors, and panels ordered from builders' catalogs. The new house, completed on Christmas Eve 1949, backed up to a concrete retaining wall along the steep hillside and faced east over the meadow.

The modular rhythm of seven-and-a-half-foot bays animates the facades and articulates the volumes of house (seven bays plus a south porch), patio (four), and studio (five). Both blocks are 20 feet wide and 17 feet high. In the 1,500-square-foot house, a sleeping gallery with sliding screens overlooks a nearly cubic living room; tucked in below are a seating nook, a kitchen, and a dining room. The 1,000-square-foot studio is similarly divided. Red, blue, black, and white stucco panels and the grid of slender columns and glazing bars turn the exterior into a three-dimensional Mondrian, screened by eucalyptus trees. The taut skin serves as mirror and sponge, reflecting trunks and foliage, displaying shadows, and absorbing the dappled light through windows and fibreglass screens. Doors and windows slide open to admit the ocean breezes.

Charles and Ray Eames celebrate the completion of the structural steel skeleton.

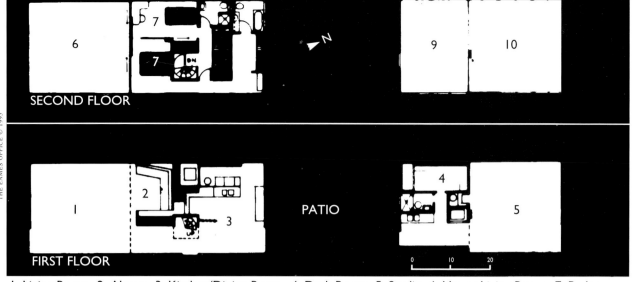

SECOND FLOOR

6

7

7

9

10

N

FIRST FLOOR

1

2

3

PATIO

4

5

0   10   20

1. Living Room 2. Alcove 3. Kitchen/Dining Room 4. Dark Room 5. Studio 6. Upper Living Room 7. Bedrooms
8. Dressing Room 9. Storage 10. Upper Studio

In the early 1960s Ray said: "The structure long ago ceased to exist. I am not aware of it." The genius of the house lies in its fusion of art and technology, container and contained, the natural and the man-made. Nothing is disguised, and there is a simple beauty in the exposed steel frame, ribbed board ceiling, linoleum floor, birch-strip rear wall, and a sculptural spiral stair ordered from a marine catalog. The house expresses the complementary skills of its makers:

Charles's love of order and process, Ray's of color, texture, and pattern. Like the furniture they were designing at that time—notably the wire-framed fiberglass chair and the modular storage units—it is economical, witty, and inventive.

In the 30 years they shared the house, every corner was filled with colorful objects from around the world, with prototypes, and with props from their films. Both were inveterate collectors; Ray was a masterly arranger. A short film, "House:

A three-dimensional Mondrian screened by eucalyptus trees.

Looking through the kitchen along the east front toward the living room.

Ray and Charles Eames in the double-height living room, beneath the sleeping gallery.

After Five Years of Living," made in 1955, captures the interplay of flowers and dolls, leaves and paper lanterns, the stair treads extending to suggest a fan, and, above all, the magical light. The house reaches out across the Pacific. Its casual, outdoor spirit is quintessentially Californian, but its quiet precision and harmony with nature evoke Japan.

Charles Moore told historian Esther McCoy: "Eames...singlehandedly brought back richness—he was the first to pull back in the wonderful things from everywhere which made the spartan framework acceptable to us." Charles Eames said of his work: "The details are not details. They make the product. It will in the end be the details that give the product its life." Forty years later, the framework and the details are lovingly maintained by the family just as Charles and Ray left them. ■

Glass House, New Canaan, Connecticut, 1946–49

IN THE SAME YEAR as the Eameses built their steel and glass pavilions, but 2,500 miles to the east, Johnson was deploying the same materials to dramatically different effect in his Glass House. It was, in a literal sense, his masterpiece; proof that his work could rival that of the architects he admired. Until then his most celebrated achievement had been the "International Style" exhibition he had co-curated with Henry-Russell Hitchcock at the fledgling Museum of Modern Art in New York in 1932. With that legendary show, which later toured the country, he helped establish a pantheon of modern masters, then unknown to the American public. Mies, Gropius, Le Corbusier, and J. J. P. Oud represented Europe; the American section included Neutra and, with many reservations, Wright. Later Johnson acquired a degree in architecture from Harvard and built a house in Cambridge as his thesis project. But, through the ups and downs in his own career, he has continued to excel as an impresario, anticipating and celebrating every shift of style, fostering new talent, and often provoking his peers.

In the late 1940s Johnson was closely associated with Mies—with whom he would work on the Seagram Building. Mies had already proposed two glass houses of his own, and, in 1950, he completed the Farnsworth House in Illinois—an exquisitely refined white-enameled steel pavilion and deck raised several feet above a water meadow. Eames backed away from a design he considered derivative; Johnson recognized how differently he could interpret "the worship of glass we had inherited from [German pioneers] Scheerbart and Taut."

"I was building an American house," he explains. "I like to get outdoors quickly, so I raised it [only] two steps above the ground. It's anchored by a brick podium and a brick cylinder that penetrates the roof plane. Mies didn't like that. His philosophy was based on uninterrupted floating planes. I was inspired by Schinkel's symmetry, as well as the big windows of Mies and his details as far as I understood them. He said: 'Some day, Philip, I'll show you how to do a corner.' That was as close as he came to chastising me."

Like so many other famous buildings that are familiar from photographs (including the Farnsworth House), the Glass House underwhelms at first sight. It is set on a promontory overlooking a lake Johnson created when he began to landscape his 40 acres, and it is framed by drystone walls that were built when the land was farmed. In form and siting it suggests a temple. Slim black columns rise from the podium to support a strong entablature; within you can glimpse twin goddesses (maquettes for Elie Nadelman's lobby sculpture in Johnson's New York State Theatre). At the Farnsworth House, drapes are drawn to protect artworks, sealing it off. The Eames House is part transparent, part opaque. The Johnson House is entirely transparent but for one cluster of moveable shades, and from a distance it suggests a ruin or an open-sided gazebo. Johnson was inspired not only by Mies's geometry and Schinkel's neo-classical temples but by a wartime memory of a wooden village that had burned, leaving only the masonry elements standing. "Over my chimney I slipped a steel cage with a glass skin," he says.

Within the 32 x 56-foot space, dining, sitting, and sleeping areas, plus a kitchen counter, the desk, and the goddesses are disposed assymetrically around the chimney, which also contains the bathroom. Jokes have been made about the need to keep everything in its place, but the interior feels almost cozy after the obsessive order of the Farnsworth house, with its built-in spine separating the different functions. There, you remove your shoes to avoid marking the travertine floors; here, everything floats free, doors slide open on all four sides, and leaves drift in across the herringbone-brick floor. There is a zen-like elimination of the inessential; you can almost imagine the owner

Philip Johnson at his monument to Lincoln Kirstein; beyond is the miniature temple in the lake and the house above. Overleaf: The house suggests a steel and glass temple set on a brick podium. (© NORMAN McGRATH)

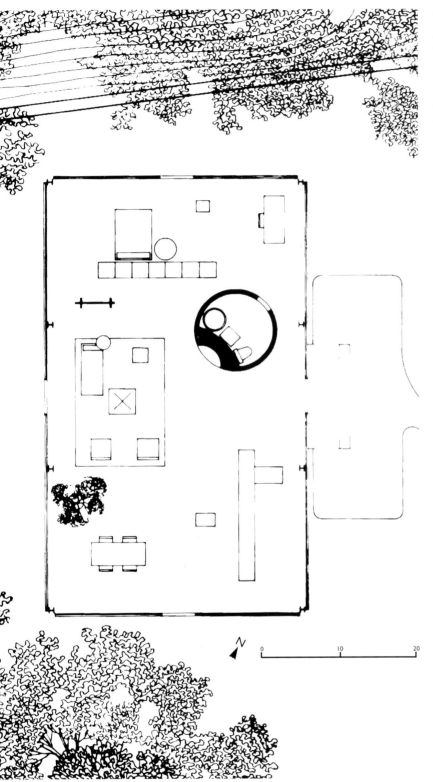

raking the gravel drive to suggest a rippling ocean.

"It's often written about as a house you cannot live in," says Johnson. "I don't know why—I've been going there for nearly 45 years. Over the last ten years I've spent almost every weekend there, in all seasons; in fog, snow, and moonlight. It gets a little cold in winter, and warm in summer—but the doors give cross ventilation. You adapt."

From the unchanging Glass House, invisible axes extend to an eclectic galaxy of satellite buildings and follies. Close by is the impassive brick guest house; to the northeast an art gallery, buried in a tumulus, and the glass-roofed, whitewashed brick vortex of the sculpture gallery. To the south, amid long grass that discourages casual callers, is a one-person study, like a tiny white chapel, lit from a roof cone. Below the promontory is an underscaled lake pavilion and a stepped tower of concrete blocks dedicated to Lincoln Kirstein, guiding spirit of the New York City Ballet. As Vincent Scully wrote: "His place now joins, as no one thirty years ago could ever have thought it would, not only Taliesin West but Monticello too as a major memorial to the complicated love affair Americans have with their land." ■

Philip Johnson has willed his New Canaan estate to the National Trust for Historic Preservation, which will eventually open it to the public as one of its historic properties.

Trees reflected in the glass around the sparely furnished sleeping area.

Living and dining areas. There is a zen-like elimination of the inessential.

Santa Monica, California, 1977–78; 1987–94

FRANK GEHRY is the maverick in a Brooks Brothers shirt, an artist-architect who, after 30 years of struggle for quality jobs and public respect, has won it all but is still tormented by self doubts and by every shaft of criticism. He was given the Pritzker Prize, architecture's equivalent of the Nobel award; he has designed Walt Disney Concert Hall, which promises to be the most exciting building in Los Angeles; and he is on the "A" list for prestigious commissions around the world. "Frank is unique...in his passion for using strange shapes and giving you a gut reaction that no-one else succeeds in doing," said Philip Johnson in a 1982 *New York Times* interview. "His buildings are shocking...but they give you a mysterious feeling of delight. I wish one could get into words or pictures that double sense of space he's able to get several times in his own house."

That house is a self-portrait, begun when work and money were scarce; an icon of deconstructivism, before that term acquired currency; and a lightning rod for the hostility that always greets radical departures from convention. Gehry's wife, Berta, found a small pink cottage on a quiet residential street, and Frank decided to wrap a new house around the old— adding 800 square feet to the existing 2,100—to achieve "a tension between the two...and to layer space from the exterior to the darker interior." The materials he chose for his wrap-around were corrugated metal, chain-link fencing, and unfinished plywood. The neighbors were as scandalized as if he had strolled past their doors in his underwear. In vain, he pointed out that they used those same materials for the boats and trailers parked in their drives, to fence their yards, and to wall their garages. One woman tried to sue; someone fired a shot through his window—though Gehry later discovered that the culprit lacked aesthetic conviction: he had also fired at other, quite inoffensive houses.

Time and Nancy Goslee Power's garden have softened the impact, but the house is still arresting. Gehry insists he was simply "trying to build a lot of ideas. Buildings under construction look nicer than buildings finished...how could a building be made to look like it's in process?...That's what led me to explore opening up the structure and using the raw wood techniques...." A friend of

leading Los Angeles artists, he was impressed by the immediacy of a brush stroke on a bare canvas and tried to capture that spontaneity and sense of improvisation in his work. Finally, the roughness of materials and finishes, here and in other projects of that time, was an honest reflection of meager budgets. "Cheapskate architecture," he called it.

The steel carapace extended back from the house to wall the yard, with a tilted cut-out to frame a giant cactus. Wood-framed glass cubes spilled out and were echoed in angled planes of chain link. Within the house, Gehry stripped stucco walls to their frames and removed the upstairs ceiling to reveal the roof structure. The kitchen-dining room was floored in asphalt. Light entered from every angle; glass revealed and reflected; the entire composition felt as though it were in motion. Everything was stripped and layered, exploded and fractured. You walked in and out of the old house and the new. As Wright expostulated to Johnson when he visited the Glass House: "Am I outdoors or in? Do I take my hat off or keep it on?"

After ten years of aesthetic delight and practical inconveniences—especially the noisy acoustics—Frank and Berta and their two growing sons decided they needed more and better insulated space. In 1987, Gehry made elaborate plans for expansion, and he later considered underground

extensions. Squeezed by budgetary constraints and increasingly restrictive building regulations and by the pressures of an expanding practice, he didn't begin work until 1992. Suddenly he realized how attached he was to the old house. "I didn't want to change it, but I had to," he admits. "I'm going to sweeten it up for privacy. All the good stuff has gone—it was like unraveling a sweater."

He exaggerates. There are new delights to compensate for the loss of the old. Nancy Power has designed a garden that shelters a breakfast terrace beside the street entrance; within is a joke fountain—three faucets plopping water into a basin—that pays homage to a scene in Jacques Tati's *Mon Oncle*, a movie that parodied the excesses of modernism. Wooden battens now conceal the exposed rafters, and the living room that once had a conversation pit has been levelled.

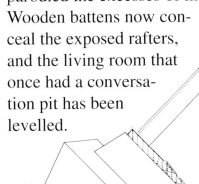

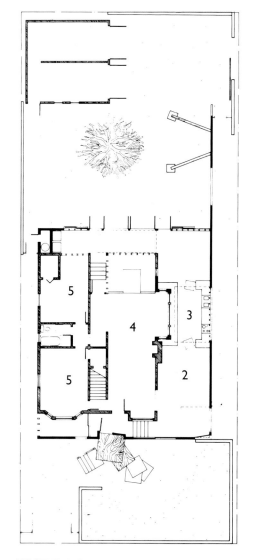

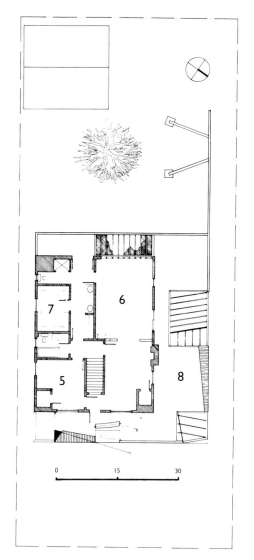

FIRST FLOOR
1. Entry 2. Dining 3. Kitchen 4. Living 5. Bedrooms

SECOND FLOOR
6. Master Bedroom 7. Closet 8. Deck

But Gehry plans to cut a hole in the floor for a coiled glass snake ascending towards a skylight-table in the master bedroom above. The house has been extended into the back yard to add a bedroom and storage; the garage has been turned into a playhouse. Between the house and garage is a pool. In the bedroom, an insert of tempered glass has replaced a walkway of chain link beyond the frame of the old house. Stairs lead up to a new attic study-library, with windows that are barred with old studs, and out to a terrace that commands sweeping views, on the rare haze-free day, of ocean and mountains.

Family and neighbors are happy. Gehry claims to be unhappy— but is dreaming of moving out and resuming his experiments in a smaller house, leaving the old in charge of his sons when they have grown. Like Wright and Johnson, he is constantly renewing his inspiration, and he is still dedicated to the notion that process is as important as the product. ■

The shock of the new (above) has been softened by Nancy Power's garden (below).

45

A wood-framed glass cube projects from the kitchen, located in the addition.

Living room, furnished with Gehry's cardboard chairs, at the core of the original house.

Austin, Texas, 1986–87

OVER THE PAST 35 YEARS, Charles Moore has collaborated with an extended family of architects across the United States to create a legion of joyful buildings, from the Sea Ranch condominiums in Mendocino County, California, to the Tegel Harbor housing complex in Berlin. As a professor of architecture at Berkeley, then at Yale, UCLA and the University of Texas, and as a collaborator, he has communicated his love of history and the vernacular; of color, collage, and playful complexity. "As an absorber of images and influences," he once declared, "I operate between the soaking action of a sponge and the gulp of a piranha." Erudite, exuberant, and prolific, he is best known as a maker of and writer on houses. "They have given me the freedom to try new ideas," he says. "If I don't like what I've done, I move on." His latest, a joint project with partner Arthur Andersson, was built when Moore joined the faculty in Austin.

It is outwardly unremarkable, almost concealed by trees on a leafy street. Shed-like buildings with plain boarded walls and pitched tin roofs suggest a farm in the surrounding hill country. Steps lead down from a gate tower past a square design studio to a courtyard with lap pool, pergolas, and a fountain. Andersson's house sits at an angle to Moore's.

For himself, Moore began with an existing ranch house that was undistinguished yet pretentious—"something a minor mafioso might have established for his paramour in 1936," as he described it. Working with Andersson and Richard Dodge, he hollowed out the shell, but kept most of the small sash windows and much of the roof. The 2,300-square-foot plan is very simple: essentially a broad hall set at right angles to a large living room. In contrast to his tight-packed, vertical Los Angeles house, all the principal rooms are on the ground floor. The master bedroom, with its tin-lined, skylit bathroom, leads out of the hall; a lofty solarium juts from the living room. Narrow steps, at the entrance and in the solarium, lead up to lofts that double as guest bedrooms.

Mies believed that "less is more." Moore has a taste for reckless profusion, and argues that "you must expose your dreams and fantasies." Here, as in all his houses, the container and the contained are interdependent. Rich colors, cut-out shapes, and a magpie hoard enrich every

MICHAEL WEBB

surface. Shifts of level and hidden openings transform what looks simple on paper into a magical labyrinth. A curved screen wall and hollow pilasters cut through entrance hall and living room, separating private areas from public, and layering space—as Moore had done with a pair of mock-classic aedicules, or framed shrines, in his first house, 25 years earlier. The curve leads you forward—a colleague likened it to the experience of paddling a canoe along a curving, high-banked stream. It extends outside as garden wall, tracing what ranchers would call a "lazy O" on the plan.

Walking through, the owner points to lines in the floor that mark the original porch and bedrooms, as though he had excavated a ruin. "Incorporating the old fabric had more to do with archeology than frugality because it ended up costing more," he admits. He has lovingly preserved the pattern of mastic tiles,

Gate tower inspired by a California ranch.

removed from the concrete floor, alongside a bold painted pattern of squares and circles that ties the interior together. The kitchen has been newly panelled in faux-marble Formica to resemble an illustration in a late 1950s *House Beautiful*. "I'm very proud of that," he beams.

Moore is an obsessive collector. "I thought I had enough space for everything in this house, but I forgot how much was in storage," he confesses. On display is a town built from carved wooden models he bought from a peddler in Mexico, a menagerie of sun-bleached wood animals, and an army of tin soldiers. Kachina dolls preside over the pilasters. Books have spread everywhere; there is a month's reading in the bathroom alone. Challenged to identify the first thing he would save from a fire, he picks the early-19th-century portraits of his great-great-grandparents, which have accompanied him on every move.

"After seven years, this still feels the most comfortable of the eight houses I've built for myself," says Moore. "It is like a sketch that is constantly evolving as you add another line here, another color there." He is constantly adding: a new drafting room, a garden, an elaborate cuttin gate. Every shelf is full, but he cannot stop collecting. ∎

Charles Moore died as this book was going to press.

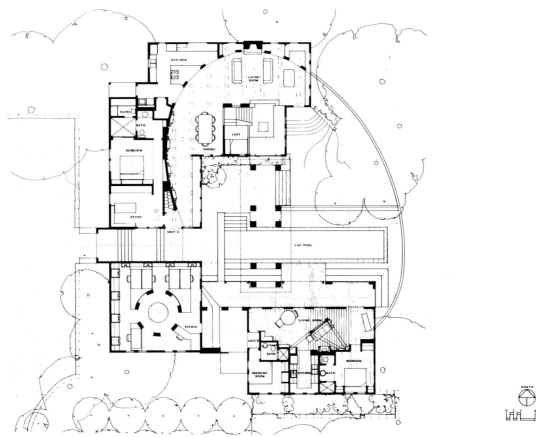

Below: Courtyard with lap pool and pergolas links the houses of Moore and Andersson with their studio.

Overleaf: Curved screen wall that leads you through the house. (OBERTO GILI / © 1988 CONDE NAST PUBLICATIONS)

Branford, Connecticut, 1979–80

TOURISTS STROLLING the streets of this picturesque coastal village often mistake the Simon-Bellamy house for a church. Sandwiched between mature trees on a narrow lot, it plays a supporting role to the big Queen Anne across the street. "New England is about verticality," says Mark Simon, "and this is a simple box that is puffing itself up, like a butterfly emerging from a chrysalis."

Simon was trained as a sculptor, like his father, then studied architecture under Charles Moore at Yale. He worked as a cabinetmaker before joining the firm of Moore Grover Harper (now Centerbrook Architects) in 1974. "I struggled to find my own voice," he recalls and he did. But on this, his first project, the influence of Moore shows in the erudite whimsy, inventive compression, and even the language he used to describe the house: "Here a curved mansard dome, recalling one atop a notable neighbor, joins with windows and stickwork at the front deck to become a giant ornament. Thus decorated, our ordinary gabled box dreams of being a captain-of-industry mansion."

It began as a simple 1910 bungalow. Instead of tearing it down, Simon decided to save the walls and oak floors, remove

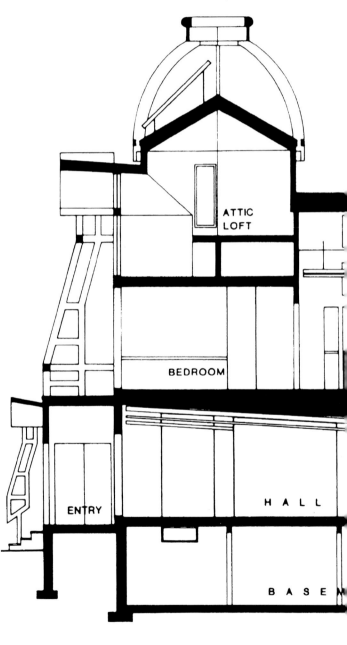

the roof and add a second story. Two splayed front porches lead the eye up to the tower, which is rotated at 45 degrees to the house, and crowned with a lattice dome that frames a solar collector. Throughout he achieves a civilized dialogue between old and new, context and innovation. "Today I might do it more delicately and less exuberantly," he says. "However, I don't worry about resale; this is a town that is full of crazy houses."

An axial hall extends 35 feet from front to back door. The walls taper, and

Sleeping alcove tucked beneath stairs to attic story.

Tapered hall merges with the living room to left.

Library inspired by Sir John Soane's inventive use of space in his house in London.

LOFT

BEDROOM

MUD ROOM

T

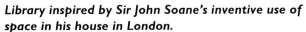

5

SECTION

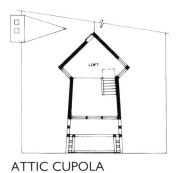

ATTIC CUPOLA

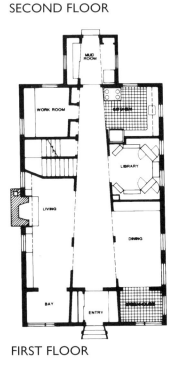

SECOND FLOOR

FIRST FLOOR

the ceiling drops from nine to seven feet to force the perspective and make the 2,000-square-foot interior feel much grander than it is—a device that was a favorite of baroque architects. Simon's wife, Penny Bellamy, who is an attorney, wanted separate living and dining rooms, a study, and a library. Simon treated each of these and a greenhouse beside the porch as alcoves opening off the hall, which links and enlarges them. Each room has its special character. Wavy ribbons of wood and masonite are suspended over the living room, and the dining room has an oval vault. The library, eight feet across, borrows ideas from Sir John Soane's house in London to create two swiveling bookcases and a dome that is studded with tiny mirrors and bicycle reflectors.

Stairs lead up to a similar wedge hall. The parents' bed is tucked in between wall and the steep stair to the tower, like Jefferson's sleeping alcove at Monticello. The daughter's room has a loft space; the son's was added as a gable at the back after the house was built. Color is used boldly: earth red and cornflower blue are set off by softer tones. "I learned from Moore that small spaces are interesting, and I squeezed things more here than I would have for a client," says Simon. "But it's a wonderfully friendly house that accepts clutter cheerfully and has adapted as our children grew." ■

Opposite: "A simple house that is puffing itself up."

Encino, California, 1992–93

IN THE MOVIES, creatures from outer space have a special affection for the San Fernando Valley. It's conveniently close to several major studios, generically mid-American in its alternation of malls and tract housing, and spookily devoid of street life. Just the place for E.T. and other extra-terrestrials to pass unnoticed. In real life it is one of the last bastions of affordable single-family houses within easy reach of Los Angeles, mountains, and ocean.

Raquel Vert and her husband, Chaim Meital, bought such a house while she was taking her master's degree in architecture at UCLA and he was launching his practice as a veterinarian. For the first 12 years, she was too absorbed in pace-setting projects for Frank Gehry, Morphosis, and Craig Hodgetts, and in raising two small children, to worry about home improvement. "Then Chaim asked me why I never invited my friends to the house," she recalls. "It was the beginning of the recession; I had established my own office, but work was slow. Chaim said: 'I have a job for you. You can remodel this house if you stick to the budget and design something we can resell.'"

Vert decided to stay within the footprint of the original house but extend it upward to give height to the living areas and to create a new second-floor master bedroom suite and a studio over the garage. All but a corner of the old struc-ture, with its wood siding and shingled roof, would be refaced in steel-troweled stucco. She built a model to show her husband, who said: "Go ahead and surprise me." Challenged to create a 5,500-square-foot house at minimum cost, she spent three months locating a builder who could interpret her drawings and work under her direction, using inexpensive materials and standard fittings.

The house occupies a gently sloping site at the foot of the ridge that divides the San Fernando Valley from Los Angeles. Vert preserved the mature trees that shelter the house from the street and the fierce summer sun, permitting her to introduce large expanses of glass on the south front to balance light from the big north windows which overlook the garden. Schindler inspired the mitered-glass corners and angled planes; Gehry was a model for the inventive use of rough materials. Vert infused the house with the strength and mystery of her native Jerusalem, creating a work of great originality with the simplest of means.

Split concrete-block walls conceal the steps down to the entry, enclose the forecourt, and flow through a sheet of glass that is wrapped around the base of the lofty entry hall. Stairs, a guest bathroom, and the vaulted dining room are all concealed by folded planes of gray stucco, jointed to suggest massive blocks of masonry—a device that is repeated around the living room fireplace. Every room, every shift of level evokes the spatial intricacy of a house in the rebuilt Jewish Quarter of Jerusalem combined with the lofty, open, light-filled volumes of Southern California modernism. Walls and ceilings are cut away to bring light into the heart of the house and to achieve a free flow of space.

The best architects know where to save and where to spend. Recessed down- and up-lights, bought off the shelf at a local hardware store, play off the rough textures of the walls and the fir studs that arch 20 feet over the central dining room. Gray Italian limestone was bought in bulk for the floors and counters in the kitchen and master bathroom; the gutsy grain of industrial-grade oak floors, birch plywood cabinets, and fir joinery needs no ornament. In back, an angular stair of perforated steel emerges from between two glass bays to link dining room and garden. Vert's one indulgence is her collection of Italian designer chairs and light fittings—bought, she insists, when the dollar was strong—and a few meticulously detailed pieces she is planning to build herself.

"I wish I could have been more daring," she says, "instead of having to create something everyone would like. But the budget demanded a minimalist aesthetic—which is what I prefer. And I put in the steel stair to break the calmness." In fact, she has breached most of the conventions of suburban housing without losing touch with practicality. Her first major built project, the house began as a pragmatic exercise and evolved into a statement of principle: a demonstration of what she hopes to achieve for future clients. ■

MICHAEL WEBB

© DOUGLAS HILL

The arched wooden vault of the dining room is visible at night from the garden.

Glass and concrete block intersect in the entry hall; stairs lead up to the study.

GROUND FLOOR
1. Front Deck
2. Entrance
3. Dining
4. Kitchen
5. Guest Bath
6. Living Room
7. Bar
8. Garage
9. Bedrooms

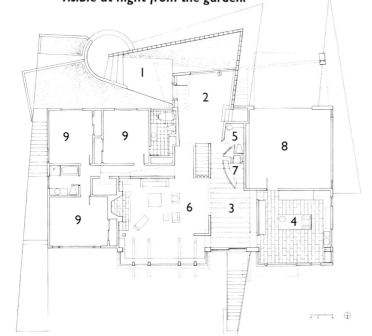

The living room and hearth are animated by light from above.

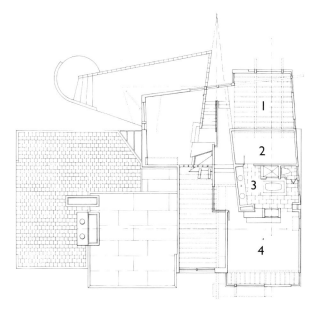

UPPER FLOOR
1. Studio
2. Closet
3. Master Bath
4. Master Bedroom

Chappaqua, New York, 1977–

"WHITE IS WONDERFUL to live with, such a hospitable color—I never get tired of it," says Susan Kroeger, who administers her husband's architectural office four blocks from their house in the Westchester County village of Chappaqua. Keith had worked for Ulrich Franzen before moving here to start his mainly residential practice. The Kroegers searched for something tumble-down that he could work on—hoping for, but not daring to expect, something rural—and found the place of their dreams: a decrepit 1879 cow barn, with burst pipes, that had been awkwardly converted to a guest house. The bank was as happy as they; it had been trying for two years to unload this wreck.

Unlike Mr. Blandings, Mr. Kroeger had no intention of turning his find into a suburban dream house. Rather, he worked at it like a sculptor with a block of stone,

Keith and Susan Kroeger with their vintage Pegasus sign, which they have mounted on their garage.

carving away to find the beauty concealed within. "I had always coveted a New York City loft—so this became our loft in suburbia," he explains. "We already had our cozy nest—a shingled vacation cottage in Maine. I couldn't bear to live that way all the time."

The barn offered several advantages. It sat on a hillside, giving easy access to its three floors; it had been previously approved for habitation, so there were no building inspections; best of all it was conveniently close to the road. "You couldn't build it now," laughs Kroeger. "It's in total violation of the current code, which shows how wrong-headed the regulations are."

They spent almost every weekend for eighteen months, "removing, removing wherever possible," until they had a bare shell, which they insulated, reconfigured and painted white. Not just the walls, but the floor, vault, beams, stairs to the

MICHAEL WEBB

The remodelled 1879 cow barn is framed by the pool pergola.

A skylight intensifies the light over the bed and the rough white surfaces.

Stairs lead up to the master bedroom.

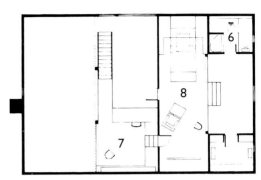

UPPER LEVEL
7. Study 8. Master Bedroom

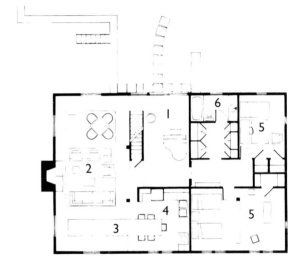

ENTRY LEVEL
1. Entry 2. Living 3. Dining 4. Kitchen 5. Bedroom
6. Bath

►N

LOWER LEVEL
9. Library 10. Laundry

Opposite: Loft-like main floor with twig sculpture.

mezzanine, and the interior shutters that cover the windows at night are white. Bed sheets, slipcovers, tables, and sofas are—white. It is the whitest house you have ever seen, a wonderful set for a movie about heaven. It explodes with light and focuses attention, like an invisible lens, on things you would overlook in a conventional interior. Every speck of color, and especially the vintage Mobil Pegasus mounted on the garage and framed by the living room window, glows with the intensity of neon. Susan is passionate about her garden; Keith's twig sculptures—and a stack of logs—bring that spirit indoors.

The 4,000-square-foot house is organized vertically. The lowest floor, still aromatic from manure, shelters mechanical equipment; the next has an axial corridor linking a library with guest bedrooms. The library is a place to display treasures—a magnetic assemblage of flatware by Vito Acconci, and a Piranesi print of the Roman Forum, looking much better with vegetation and sheep than it does today.

Above is the main floor, loft-like in its openness and its 28-foot-high vault. The kitchen is a part of the living-dining room and can comfortably accommodate any number of people. Unrailed steps lead up to a bridge-mezzanine that feels suspended in space. Master bedroom, bathroom, and dressing areas are separated by a few steps. A skylight over the bed provides an intensity of light that evokes Renaissance paintings of the Annunciation. "It's my favorite place to go camping, and it's right next to my own bathroom," says Susan.

When your eyes have adjusted to the brightness of the interior, you begin to notice its subtleties: the sense of axiality that organizes the parts on each level; the way the volumes interlock; the rough edge to the purity—this is cow heaven, not a Syrie Maugham penthouse. "Now the children have grown we have it to ourselves," says Keith. "It has proved so absorbing, we can't tear ourselves away, and there are still things to be changed." ∎

RICHARD FERNAU (1946–)

Berkeley, California, 1989–92

RICHARD FERNAU has won acclaim for the inventive, site-specific buildings, especially houses, that he has designed over the past 14 years with partner Laura Hartman. But the budget for his own place was tight, and a colleague at Berkeley, where he teaches architecture, advised: "Swallow your pride and buy a house that no-one wants—but with good windows." Fernau's wife, attorney Sarah Cunniff, found the ugly duckling on a leafy hill road above the Berkeley campus. "Even the windows were bad," recalls the architect. "It had been built in the 1950s as a dependency of the house next door—one big room over a garage—and had been extended and 'modernized' in the 1970s. But it had good bones."

The house stood close to the road, shunning its chief asset: a creek to the rear, full of mature cypress, fir, and redwood trees. Fernau quickly realized that he should strip the house of its accretions, open up the back and add rooms below street level, but he took his time to decide exactly how to do these things. Limited funds, a tight footprint, and the steep slope were challenges. "Our firm often builds houses on spectacular coastlines and mountains," says the architect. "It almost takes breathing exercises not to go over the top, and to do what's appropriate for the client and the site. Here it was a matter of doing a few things well—like a chef whipping up a great meal from whatever happens to be in the kitchen."

The October 1989 earthquake shook down the brick chimney and spurred him to start. Out came the unsightly aluminium window frames, the acoustic drop ceiling in the living room, and the marbleized mirror glass in the bedroom to the rear. He added a straight stair up to a partially-closed entry porch and turned the rear bedroom into a study-porch with awning windows on two sides. Below, he added a master bedroom opening onto a sleeping deck, and a bedroom for his small son at the lowest level, partly excavated from the hillside. Two elements—a redwood log and a stair tower—tie this stack of spaces together.

The 16-foot-long, 3,000-pound log was a present from a contractor with whom he had built a student union at the University of California at Santa Cruz. It was delivered to his doorstep and sat

MICHAEL WEBB

there until he decided to use it as a column to support the cantilevered study and brace the sleeping deck. His builder, justifiably anxious about moving this unwieldy object where there was no access for a crane, tried to talk him out of it. He called on a friend, a former zen priest who specializes in building with old timber, to devise a way of installing it safely—which he agreed to do in exchange for a good party. The log was rolled down the slope on a trolley and ramp and winched into position in its concrete socket-base as though the team were raising a circus big top.

The vertical skylit stair tower brings light and air to the center of the house, and its creamy yellow walls cast a glow into the adjoining rooms. Fernau loves color, and he enjoyed the opportunity of playing with 16 tones of red, yellow, green, and blue. The colors animate doors and window frames, eaves and reveals, highlighting the dark shingles of the facade. Paler colors are brushed on thinly to allow the natural redwood boards to emerge. "It was fun to try them out full-scale,"

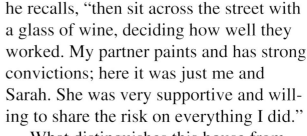

he recalls, "then sit across the street with a glass of wine, deciding how well they worked. My partner paints and has strong convictions; here it was just me and Sarah. She was very supportive and willing to share the risk on everything I did."

What distinguishes this house from others he has done is the combination of openness and modest scale. It contains 1,650 square feet, but many of the spaces are partly enclosed or uninsulated, accepting winter chill to exploit the balmy days of summer and the crisp air of spring and fall. The owners sleep outdoors for most of the year, sliding a bright yellow door out into space and rolling their caster-mounted Finn-ply bed onto the deck. But there is a price to pay. "When you take a design like this to an appraiser, it's like a medical exam," Fernau complains. "Half the rooms in this house don't meet his criteria."

The house combines the virtues of a bohemian retreat and a Shaker cabinet, loose yet impeccably crafted. It embraces the landscape, making the foliage, soft redwood bark, and gurgling creek an integral part of daily life. "It's a joy to live in a well-designed house," says Fernau, "where everything is ordered and in the right place; to enjoy the breezes, the play of light, and the constant surprises. Making it has restored my faith in the power of architecture." ∎

Opposite: A redwood log supports a cantilevered study and braces the sleeping deck above a creek.

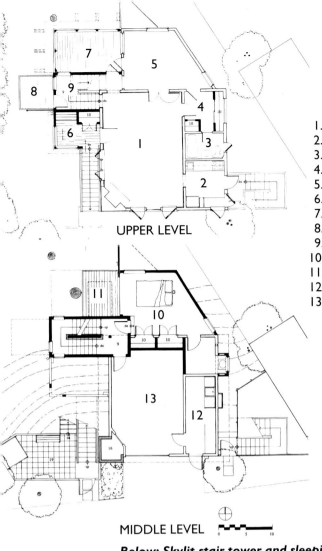

UPPER LEVEL

1. Living / Dining
2. Kitchen
3. Bathroom
4. Hall
5. Den
6. Entry Porch
7. Study Porch
8. West Deck
9. Stair Tower
10. Master Bedroom
11. Sleeping Porch
12. Utility Room
13. Garage

MIDDLE LEVEL

Below: Skylit stair tower and sleeping porch.

Above: Corner of the study-porch.

Round Hill, Woodbridge, Connecticut, 1982–83

A PAVILION that would capture light and breezes and command a view: that was Herbert Newman's goal once his children had grown. His wife, Edna, craved sunlight; he wanted a retreat that was close to his practice in New Haven and his classes at the Yale School of Architecture. On a trip to Europe they admired Palladio's Villa Rotunda and Chiswick House, a Palladian miniature near London. Like Jefferson, the Newmans sought the glorious isolation of a hilltop. They found the ideal site, 650 feet above sea level, overlooking mature trees, with a distant prospect of Long Island across the Sound and the tip of New Haven's tallest tower to remind them where they were. It gave its name to the house: Round Hill.

Glacial gravel was excavated to create a circular entrance court and to frame a circular pool (for reflections and swimming) to the south. The house is centered on the axis between these two circles, which are echoed in a series of round windows. A 16-foot-square steel-framed tower, capped with a pyramid roof, emerges from a two-story brick hall with bevelled corners. Wood-framed wings, clad in plywood and ornamented with a four-foot grid of battens, open off this hall at first and second floor levels. Soon to come is a glass-walled library—a skeletal temple extending from the southwest corner.

The house presents a closed face to the north, for protection against winter winds, but it opens up to the south, where pergolas reach out to embrace the landscape. They create, with the trellis wrapped around the tower, a lacy grid that dematerializes the structure. It resembles a big gazebo more than a Palladian villa; classical in its symmetry, modern in its lightness and transparency. A gleaming object by day, a glowing lantern at night, the house has a joyful, quirky character, and its 3,500-square-foot interior is surprisingly intimate.

"I've always been fascinated by the layering of space and the filtering of light," says Newman. "I was a student of Louis Kahn's at Yale, and I've tried to articulate light and space as he did, but without his fear of symmetry and axiality." The entry hall, with its circular openings revealing the deck and trellis around

MICHAEL WEBB

the tower, and its stair swooping up from one opening to vanish above the ceiling, suggests a playful tribute to the monumental vault in Kahn's Yale Center for British Art. There, you feel you are in an ancient ruin; here in an ethereal bird cage, so bright and exuberant are the white walls and oak trim. Adding to the fun is the play of geometric forms: the inner volume of the tower opening into the 24-foot square of the hall; triangular openings playing off circles and squares.

The view from the hill, held back by the impassive entrance facade, bursts upon you as you step through the front door. The bowed glass window of the living room pulls you outside, and the light animates every corner of the house. "It's never too bright," says Newman, "but the midday sun bounces through the house like a stone skipping over the surface of a pond, and when it's snowy outside

the interior starts to dance."

The third-floor belvedere feels detached from the rest of the house—a retreat within a retreat. It's a place for drinks at sunset, or to dream away a sultry afternoon, refreshed by breezes off Long Island Sound. The trellis balustrade and the cedar deck give the house the feel of a seaside cottage, sparing the Newmans a long drive to a second home.

The erudite wit of the design is matched by an eclectic choice of art works: a sketch of Borromini's S. Ivo in Rome by a former colleage at I. M. Pei; tiny terra-cotta houses from the Caribbean island of Nevis; a painting by Mark Wilson that was inspired by a computer chip. But Newman's current favorite is the maquette of a bulldog, cast in concrete for his firm's addition to the Yale Bowl, that snarls menacingly over his pool. ■

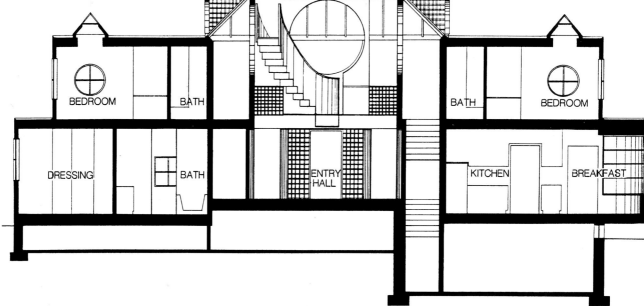

The house presents a closed face to the north, but opens up dramatically to the south.

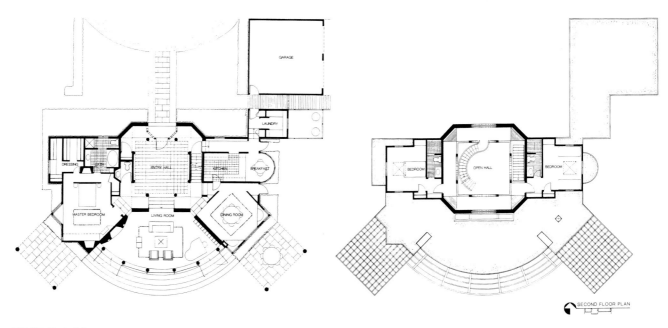

FIRST FLOOR

SECOND FLOOR

The third floor belvedere, overlooking Long Island Sound and the distant towers of New Haven.

Opposite: The stairs appear to swoop up from the second floor and vanish through the ceiling.

Malibu, California, 1987–89

"WHEN TINA AND I first moved to Southern California, we remodelled a 600-square-foot bungalow for almost no money and dreamed of building a court-yard house in close partnership with the landscape and climate," recalls Buzz Yudell. "We drove up the coast, and the only lot within our budget was a slice of hillside 600 feet long and a hundred wide. That included a dry creek; with setbacks, the house could not be wider than 32 feet."

They spent a lot of time thinking about how they wanted to live. Yudell had moved from Yale to Los Angeles with Charles Moore in 1976, and become a partner in the new firm of Moore Ruble Yudell. He shares his mentor's love of the picturesque, of architectural history, and of local building traditions. One source of inspiration was spare farm buildings, from Tuscany to Texas, that piled up simple shapes in interesting ways. He admired the sequenced spaces and harmonious proportions of Palladian villas and the way that Charles Eames breathed romance into strict geometry. "Archetypal qualities, that cut across time and style,

and a feeling of serenity were important to us," says Yudell. "Coming from the northeast, we wanted to inhale deeply and expand into the landscape, as Schindler had."

The trick was to achieve a harmonious balance of ideas and forms on the elongated site. Yudell sketched a straggly village with a path winding through and a skinny series of interlocking courtyards, but both felt forced. The final design exploited the linearity of the site instead of fighting it. Two broad north-south axes—a sun-filled gallery and a wide stone-flagged path—step down the hill and establish a symbolic link between mountains and ocean. Carefully proportioned rooms open off the gallery, which is a room in itself, broad enough for entertaining. Pergolas define garden rooms that extend west from the path and lead to Tina's jungle on the slope of the creek beyond the hedge. French windows link gallery and path at each level, establishing cross axes and a subtle layering of spaces, enclosed and open, interior and outdoors. The Spanish courtyard the owners initially craved has been absorbed within the weft and weave of house and garden.

In its 3,350 square feet (plus 1,000 in porches and a detached studio to the north), the house manipulates geometry to create a relaxed informality. The tower is a stack of three nine-foot cubes, but it feels like the turret of an old villa, especially in

Traditional farm buildings inspired the linear stack of simple forms.

The sitting room faces south toward the ocean and opens onto a porch.

Buzz's attic study. The central hearth anchors the space that flows around it and marks the shift of level from kitchen-dining to sitting rooms. There's a place for sun and shade at every time of day: porches and pergolas for breakfast, lunch, and (on warm nights) dinner.

Tina Beebe has created a complex garden from a bare hill in less than three years and, as a professional colorist, has given the house a timeless patina, using integrally colored plaster inside and out. "I called in an Italian plasterer, thinking he would understand what I needed," she recalls. "He arrived in a black Corvette, wearing a gold chain, and when I started to explain we wanted faded colors, he said: 'Lady, forget it!' and left. I made friends with the Mexican laborers and mixed trial batches, since I couldn't tell what color it would be when it dried. By trial and error we got it right."

The faded terra cotta of the outer walls matches the exposed clay on the hillside, and plays off the silvery tone of the standing-seam metal roofs, which were inspired by farms in northern California. The subtly tinted white interior has inlays and friezes in pale colors; a few areas are sky blue and green—for contrast and to help pull together the owners' mix of old and new furniture. Door frames and the pergolas take their cue from the gray-green native foliage.

It is hard to believe the house is so new and that it's a short drive from the frenzy of the coast highway. As the afternoon light streams through the house and the scents drift in from the garden, it's easy to conjure the age-old spirit of Provence, so like this land in light, colors and topography, and to imagine that the misty blue beyond the pool must be the Mediterranean. "We were concerned the house might be too spare and understated to be entirely satisfying," reflects Buzz. "There's risk as well as excitement when you are shaping your own lives. But it has turned out to be picturesque and quietly sybaritic." Above all, it demonstrates that modern ideas and traditional forms can happily co-exist. ∎

Opposite: The gallery is a room in itself, broad enough for entertaining.

GROUND FLOOR
1. Entry 2. Gallery 3. Guest Bedroom
4. Kitchen/Dining 5. Living

SECOND FLOOR
1. Guest Bedroom/Tower above 2. Study 3. Library
4. Open to Gallery Below 5. Master Bedroom
6. Dressing Room 7. Master Bath 8. Sleeping Porch

GROUND FLOOR   SECOND FLOOR

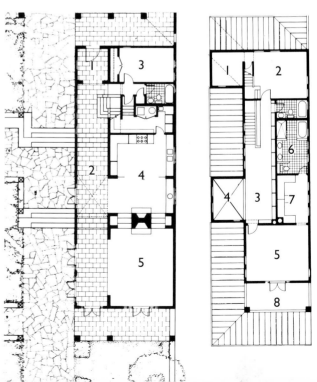

Batesville, Virginia, 1971–92

ROBERT DRIPPS AND LUCIA PHINNEY teach architecture in Thomas Jefferson's "academical village" at the University of Virginia, and its harmony, clarity, and interweaving of buildings and landscape have reinforced their convictions about the house they designed for themselves a half hour's drive to the south. When Dripps joined the faculty in 1970, he was a footloose bachelor who wanted to live in a loft. Finding none, he decided to build and discovered that 23 acres of farmland cost no more than an acre in a subdivision. He drilled a well, put in a septic tank, laid cables, and built what he calls, "an open plywood shoebox, with space for a studio, a mezzanine for sleeping and a workshop to repair my motorbikes. It was a pure-white container, simple and flexible, as neutral as possible. I felt no need of a conventional house."

In 1981, he married and formed a partnership with Lucia Phinney, with whom he shared a deep concern about the structure of cities and the relationship of buildings to the land. "Our practice has always been a means to test and validate the principles behind our teaching," he explains. "There's a strong connection between buildings and the way you live, especially for architects."

Dripps had tinkered with his box from the beginning; together he and Lucia planned a more ambitious transformation, beginning with a retaining wall that extended the house into the landscape. It was the first of many axes connecting rooms, gardens, and entry courtyard.

"We weren't prepared to tear down the box, so we rebuilt it, replacing the flat roof, plain walls, and original doors and windows," Dripps explains. "I began as a dedicated modernist and gradually realized the validity of local materials and building techniques. An architect came by to photograph 'this modern house' before it was destroyed!" In 1988, they added a second, cubic volume, housing a library and bedroom for their small son, and linked it to the first by an axial corridor-bridge at second-floor level. The exteriors use the colonial vernacular of white clapboard, black pitched roofs, and brick piers supporting porches and pergolas. Dripps and Phinney went to the source, bypassing klunky modern copies, and using the vocabulary with scholarly precision. Jefferson's Poplar Forest house inspired the porticoes at the entrance and at the northeast end.

Behind the understated facades are interiors of rare character. At the hub of the old house is a new kitchen. The product of 300 drawings, it is a friendly machine, an impeccably crafted combination of aluminium-framed maple cabinets, stainless-steel appliances, and black slate pavers. It separates the double-height living and dining rooms, with their engaging mix of rough white beams and sleek modern furniture. The dining room

Opposite: The architects in their library.

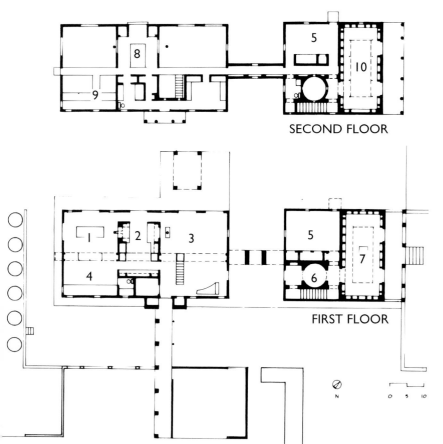

SECOND FLOOR

FIRST FLOOR

is separated from the double-deck office by a mesh screen. On the near side is an antique Chinese dresser, on the other a vintage motorbike, a last memento of carefree youth.

From the upstairs office and the master bedroom above the kitchen the axial corridor leads to the new building. The entrance rotunda beside the stairs has a conical skylight that opens into the attic,

1. Dining
2. Kitchen
3. Living
4. Office
5. Bedrooms
6. Rotunda
7. Library
8. Master Bedroom
9. Study
10. Upper Library

The exterior was inspired by Thomas Jefferson's Poplar Forest house. (ROBERT DRIPPS)

a volume within a volume. But the main event is the library, an abstraction of classical models, interpreted in contemporary materials. A steel-framed gallery of sandblasted tempered glass is cantilevered from the walls and braced with tie rods. The white grid of the balustrade echoes that of the ceiling. Blue-gray shelves support a handsome collection of architectural books.

"Monticello and the Soane house—two of our favorites—were substantially altered by their designers," notes Phinney. "Here we have changed everything but the idea." That idea—of proportion, detail and interconnection—is a thread that runs through the best architecture of every era. ∎

Above: The double-height living room is where the house began its growth, over 20 years ago.

Below: Kitchen and dining room; to the right is architects' two-level office.

JEFFERSON B. RILEY (1945–)

Guilford, Connecticut, 1976–77; 1983–86

LIKE MARK SIMON, Jefferson Riley was a student and protege of Charles Moore when he taught at Yale in the 1970s; like Simon, he helped establish the firm that is now Centerbrook Architects. But the house he built for himself and his wife, Barbara, who is a teacher, alluded to Moore and the vernacular in a less direct way. "He taught that a house should have a sense of place, and emphasized the importance of emotions, memory, and sociability," recalls Riley. "Those things were more important to me than stylistic issues."

Outcrops of the granite that was quarried for the Brooklyn Bridge and the base of the Statue of Liberty stud the wooded four-acre site, which is surrounded by state forest. Riley thought of their cozy one-room cabin in Maine, and designed a

Jefferson Riley and his daughter in a window overlooking the original family room.

1,300-square-foot clapboard house that reaches 30 feet up into the trees. Precut lumber determined its dimensions. Inspired by childhood memories of a country club in which members of staff lived in rooms that overlooked public areas, he put the bedrooms in a two-story bridge suspended within the kitchen-dining-living room, which takes on the character of an indoor piazza. The goals were to animate the space by inserting a box within a box, and to conserve energy by setting the bedroom windows back behind those in the south gable—which acts as a passive solar collector in winter and is shaded by the trees in summer.

Interior volumes produce a picturesquely massed exterior to either side of the south gable, enhanced by a stack of

dormer windows—a souvenir of the Rileys' stay in Paris—which trick you into thinking the house is five stories high. You enter through a blank wall into the screened conservatory. "I wanted a sense of threshold, the feeling you have in Charleston where you enter a house through a walled garden," says Riley. Within the kitchen-family area, an exposed stove pipe and exhaust vent carry the eye up the shaft of space; behind is a sitting area, which also looks up to the high ceiling. Vaults and walls are clad in fir boards; the floors are oak. Cherry cabinets and a stylized capital around the flue pipe are handsomely crafted.

A daughter arrived as the house was completed; soon there were also two

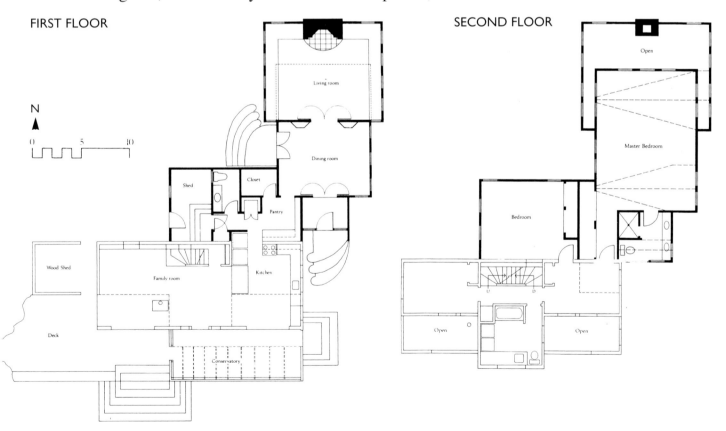

FIRST FLOOR

N

0   5   10

Wood Shed

Family room

Deck

Shed

Closet

Pantry

Kitchen

Living room

Dining room

Conservatory

SECOND FLOOR

Open

Master Bedroom

Bedroom

Open

Open

sons, leaning out of the sash windows to ask what was cooking, or tumbling down the book-lined stairs. The parents climbed another floor to their room, which projected out from the south front. "The house has fostered community, bringing the family together, but giving everyone his own turf," says the architect.

As the children grew, they needed more turf, and the parents decided to add some grown-up spaces to their cabin in the woods. Riley designed a 1,900-square-foot sequence of three gabled boxes—hall, dining, and living rooms—each larger than the other and opening out of each other on an axis. A new master suite occupies the upper floor beneath the

Above: The original unpainted clapboard house reaches 30 feet up into the trees.

Below: The painted east facade unifies the old house and the addition to the right. (© 1981 NORMAN McGRATH)

gables and is cantilevered out over the living room to within a few feet of the outer walls, creating an even more mysterious inner volume than that in the old house. A new formal entrance leads guests to a processional route around the dining table to the living room. A dog's-leg of service rooms ties the new house to the old. In the frugal New England tradition of decorating only the public facade, the east side has been painted an intense red, which effectively blurs the junction of old and new and pulls together the gables, dormers, and a bewildering array of windows.

The new rooms are more sophisticated and symmetrical than the old. A window bench with baseboard heating wraps around the formal, cherry-framed hearth. Window-filled walls are painted a soft green. The dining room has glass-fronted display cabinets and a set of Shaker chairs. The old kitchen has expanded into the link. The master bedroom has the intimacy of an attic and the serenity that comes from its layered windows, which seem to trap the early morning and late afternoon sun and the glow from embers in the hearth below. The house has evolved over two decades, but, says Riley, "some of the windows are still unpainted, so we can tell ourselves it's still not finished." ■

The symmetry of the new living room is complemented by the abundance of windows. (© 1981 NORMAN McGRATH)

WILLIAM F. STERN (1947–)

Houston, Texas, 1988–91

"ALL MY LIFE I had wanted to build a house for myself, but I had few preconceived ideas of what it should be," says William Stern, who describes himself as "a real functionalist; a fusion of American traditional and mid-century European modernism." The house William F. Stern & Associates built on a 75 x 125-foot corner lot in the leafy Montrose neighborhood uses channel-grooved cypress wood siding, broad eaves, and steel-framed sun shades to protect the soaring spaces within. Set back 25 feet to align with its 1920s neighbors, it steps back again at the southwest corner to preserve a live oak and to moderate the impact of its 43-foot height—in contrast to overscaled newcomers that shoulder up to the building line.

The house has been compared, flatteringly, to the nearby De Menil Collection, a private art museum for which Renzo Piano abstracted the residential vernacular of gray boards and white trim on a monumental scale. "Mine is different on all four sides," notes Stern. "I wanted to preserve the traditional north-south orientation and thin section, devices that were adopted before air conditioning to catch breezes and provide cross ventilation." Piano designed ceiling baffles to screen the sun while admitting natural light. Stern closed off the east and west sides, thus increasing the amount of hanging space, and opened up the interior by placing expansive windows to the north and south —where slatted cypress screens can be adjusted to block the rays in summer and winter.

"I wasn't trying to make a statement," says Stern. "But I challenged myself in a way I hadn't elsewhere, looking harder and pushing myself on all fronts to engage space. The concept came quickly, but detailed design extended over 14 months, working with an eighth-scale model. I learned a lot about myself doing this."

Stern wanted to dramatize the experience of moving through volumes that would function equally well for the display of large abstract canvases and small works on paper, for living and for entertaining. A stacked steel and maple stair rises three stories at the center of the 3,400-square-foot house, providing a ceremonial ascent. It also divides the double-height living room from the ground-floor kitchen and dining rooms and the library and guest bedroom above. Over the living room is the lofty master suite, which

opens onto a square gallery for art works. A second, more enclosed stair runs down the east wall into the entrance hall.

Each staircase provides a succession of vantage points from which to appreciate art works and the interpenetration of space within the house and beyond. Windows frame mature trees. Intimate rooms lead out of the central void; an eclectic mix of woodsy modern furniture provides a pleasing domesticity amid the grand vistas. "I love wood," says Stern, "and you see in this house instances of rough framing, finished carpentry, refined cabinets and furniture—the whole spectrum The house is raised three feet above the ground to protect it from rot and damp, and when you look out you feel you are on stage."

Most of all, Stern loves art, and his prize acquisition is a site-specific wall drawing by Sol LeWitt, a bold, room-high grid. "I wanted it as much as I wanted to build the house," says its proud owner. "LeWitt never came to the house, but his proposal picked up on the character of the framing, and it holds the whole place together."

Stern was born in Cincinnati, where his parents built a modern house that made a deep impression on him, and moved to Houston in 1976, after two years with Edward Larrabee Barnes in New York. As a newcomer, he noticed things locals overlook; for instance, how people pamper their front yards as though

PAUL HESTER

The cypress-boarded house steps back to respect its neighbors and preserve a live oak.

they were parlors but let their back yards become as messy as their dens. Stern is a perfectionist, and he decided to integrate both yards with the house, covering them with crushed granite as a setting for sculpture, and as a way of mediating between the house and the sidewalk, which he views as a neighborhood park. A low fence divides grass from gravel at the front; wild roses spill through a higher fence along the side, and a pergola links the impeccably crafted carport to the rear of the house. As a bachelor with his own firm, Stern could please himself; it's a tribute to his sensitivity and skill that he also pleased his neighbors. ■

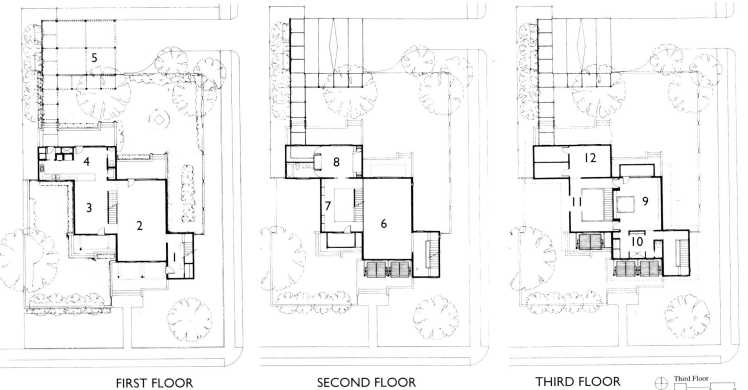

FIRST FLOOR   **SECOND FLOOR**   **THIRD FLOOR**

1. Entry 2. Living 3. Dining 4. Kitchen/Breakfast 5. Carport 6. Open to First Floor 7. Library
8. Office/Bedroom 9. Master Bedroom 10. Bath 11. Art Gallery 12. Storage

Opposite: A wall drawing by Sol LeWitt dominates the lofty living room.
Below: The steel and maple stair frames a sitting area.

Redding, Connecticut, 1991–92

BERNARD WHARTON grew up on Bermuda and loves ships, so it is no surprise that the house he built for himself, his new wife, Elaine Anthony, and their children should suggest a hull and be as trim and tightly planned as a yacht. The house distills the needs, emotions, and experience of a couple who got married on the site just before construction began. She is a painter of bold abstract canvases, and she lived for many years in Mexico. He is a partner in the firm of Shope Reno Wharton, which is best known for its expansive reinterpretations of the New England vernacular. Both are passionately attached to each other and to the rocks and trees that surround them. In the fullest sense, this was a labor of love.

"The houses we build for our clients are much grander and more conservative—up to thirty times the size of this," says Bernard. "I don't covet that. I did hundreds of sketches for this house, but kept coming back to basics. Simplicity. Practical but with a lot of whimsy. A place we felt grounded." His options were also limited by a tight budget. He laughs as he remembers the ordeal of securing a mortgage, after telling the loan officer he was self-employed, married to an artist, and paying alimony.

For Elaine, the house is suggestive of a Hansel and Gretel cottage in the woods, a corner of a French chateau, and a lodge in Maine. Bernard designed it from the inside out. The circular painting studio was influenced by forms they both liked—a kiva, a tepee, a Kentish oast house. Studios traditionally face north; here the skylight on the conical roof serves as an oculus, bathing the room in indirect light, which changes in intensity through the day. The combined kitchen-dining-living room occupies the east end of the house, which is anchored by three gables and a steel canopy over the massive rock stoop, allowing the cone to float free. At the center is the master bedroom and a gallery. Between the roof and shingled walls, tied around like a broad ribbon, is a dark green frieze of Ws and As.

The house changes its character as you move around it, from the vertical thrust of the studio, to the almost unbroken expanse of the north facade and around to the carriage doors on the south side that open each room up to the woods. "I had never designed a house without a porch," says Bernard, "but we couldn't afford to build one here. By opening up the south front, the whole house becomes a porch, and the landscape an extension of the interior."

Lofty ceilings—12 feet in the living room, 36 feet to the tip of the cone—make the house feel much larger than its modest 1,100 square feet. The house has a compression and an energy that is missing from mansions, and every space does double duty. A long table from a Mexican hacienda divides the kitchen from the sitting area; it serves for family meals, as a focus for entertaining, and as a part-time desk. Bernard and Elaine searched for special stones all over New England, finally tracking down the granite blocks for their fireplace in a remote corner of eastern Connecticut. Two steel beams form a gentle arch over the kitchen window, which frames a view out to a favorite rock. The gallery that runs past the master bedroom broadens to draw you in to the soaring vault of the studio. A ladder leads up to an attic: a bed-playroom for the boys and storage for paintings.

What makes this house special are the details: the bowed "eyelids" over the attic windows, the nautical rivets on the metal trim, the mix of fine and folk art throughout. It has the comfort of a plaid blanket hugging you tight on a chilly evening; the friendliness of a country barbecue. "Building this was fun," says Bernard. "We were the general contractors and there was a lot of sweat equity. I wanted it to look good in a hundred years, even though I won't be here to see it." ■

Bernard Wharton and Elaine Anthony.

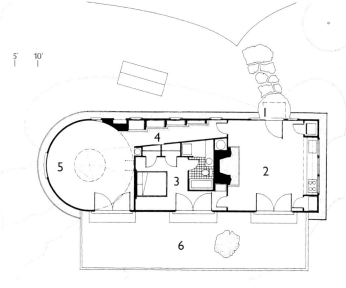

1. Entry 2. Great Room 3. Sleeping Chamber
4. Gallery 5. Studio 6. Terrace

Opposite: *Granite blocks make the hearth the focus of the kitchen-dining-living room.*

Right: *Elaine Anthony's cone-vaulted painting studio dominates the west end of the house.*

Above: *Three gables anchor the east end of the hull-like exterior.*

Overleaf: *Carriage doors on the south side open each room up to the woods.* (© H. DURSTON SAYLOR)

Houston, Texas, 1982–83

WE MAY ENVY the serenity of ancient Chinese scholars—living in the simplest of shelters, communing with nature and composing poems in exquisite calligraphy—but never hope to follow their example. Carlos Jimenez has realized that dream at the heart of a vast and chaotic city, where he has created a personal sanctuary in which he can design more buildings of refined simplicity. A tiny blue house tips its hat to the street but opens up to the north, facing a blue studio tower (a taller, slimmer version of the house) across a fenced garden that is shaded by a large pecan tree. As his practice expanded, the architect added a drafting office to the east, creating a little compound, in which each element is separate but interdependent.

"Coming from Costa Rica, I had grown up with houses that are walled off from the street, that open inwards and define territory," Jimenez explains. "This was an echo of that tradition of hard edge and soft center. The tree became a focal point and pivot in the outdoor room between house and studio—as though I was addressing an existing structure."

"Architecture is the art of listening—to your inner self and to clients," he continues in a tone of quiet intensity that compels attention. As his reputation has grown, he has stayed true to his principles; an art gallery, a printing office, and

Carlos Jimenez stands beside the bookcase that divides his pyramid-vaulted house.

houses he has built in Houston share the same qualities as his house-studio. They are direct, timeless, pared down to an essential geometry; but there is nothing cold or mechanical about these intimate volumes. Windows are precisely placed to frame trees. As the architect notes: "Houston has few points of reference. There is no ocean or mountain; even downtown is ambiguous. This enhances the value of trees, beyond their beauty and shade."

The house was his first built work. He describes it as "an intuitive project—about discovery; not a statement. A practical demonstration of my ideas of

PAUL HESTER

occupying a plot and creating shelter. Within this inexpensive cube, I strove for openness and precision, transcending its limitations." The house has the innocence of a child's first drawing, the craftsmanship of a Shaker cabinet, the purity of a zen teahouse. Within its 400 square feet are compressed everything a bachelor could want: kitchen, bathroom, living-dining room, bookshelves, and a sleeping loft.

Astonishingly, it doesn't feel compressed. The white void flows around the inner structure that supports the loft and the detached blue plane that serves as a room divider and bookcase. A red wedge conceals the bed and audio speakers. There is an echo here of early Le Corbusier villas—in the planes of color that emphasize the whiteness, the purity and plasticity of space. Jimenez acknowledges the debt. But he felt even more inspired by the spirituality and qualities of light in Louis Kahn's Kimbell Art Museum in Fort Worth.

"My buildings are designed to accommodate different uses," says Jimenez. "I want to stay here but use the spaces in different ways." Ten years after his modest start, he linked the two studios and added a mezzanine in the larger one. Now he needs more room for himself, and he plans to build a new home on an empty lot across the street, adding another dimension to the compound. But he will keep his house as a quiet place to sketch,

not least because of its superb acoustics. Sitting there in the stillness, sketch pad on his knee, with a recording of his favorite Mahler adagio wafting down from the vault, he can reflect on how his career has grown from this first seed. He recalls how "on one of those nights when clouds move across the sky like buffalo ahead of a storm, I experience a moment of repose in which I can forget the savagery of the world. Sensations like that are essential to my peace of mind." ∎

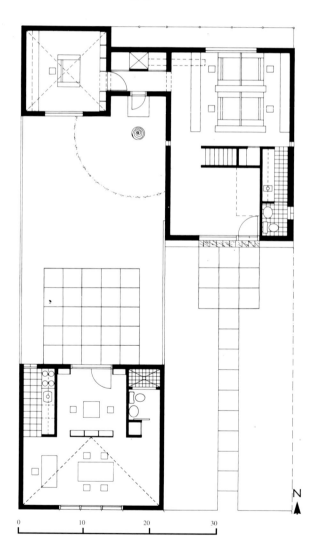

The studio tower (above) faces the house (below) across a fenced garden; to the right is the drafting office.

Winnetka, Illinois, 1982–83

THE VILLAGE OF WINNETKA resembles John Cheever territory: big traditional houses set well back on tree-lined streets, affluent executives taking the commuter train to Chicago, lots of community spirit. An unlikely place to find an uncompromising steel and glass house, but it fits right in and has won its place in a local guide, *Significant Architecture of Winnetka.*

David Hovey moved here with his wife Eileen from a high-rise Mies van der Rohe apartment in downtown Chicago. His master's thesis at the Illinois Institute of Technology (a campus designed by Mies, and still a stronghold of classic modernism) was on prefabrication; later he worked with Helmut Jahn, a maestro of steel and glass. The house he built for his family drew on these influences and the last house that Le Corbusier designed, for Heidi Weber in Zurich.

Slender steel columns and pierced sheet metal joists support two galvanized steel decks. The infill walls are made of insulated panels and glass. The frame and glazing bars are enamelled white; the red joists tie the house together visually and extend out over the side entrance and the path to a detached garage. The 30 x 60-foot rectangle contains 3,900 square feet on two floors and in the basement.

"I used industrial components and materials to show that they could be attractive, economical, and durable," says Hovey. "I wanted this house to be a model that could be mass-produced in a factory. That didn't happen, but my development and construction company now has a reputation for progressive design." The architect-engineer achieved his economies by combining standard elements with inventive treatments of inexpensive materials. The steel joists proved to be cheaper than wood, and they are all turned the same way: open to the south, closed to the north, giving the house two distinctive aspects. The front yard is partly fenced with corrugated concrete boards that were cheap to install and have survived ten winters without blemish. No-wax vinyl flooring, used for ballet studios, has withstood ten years of assault by three growing children. The stair treads, risers, and landings are formed from single sheets of 1/8-inch steel, stamped in a hydraulic press.

Solid panels provide privacy from the neighbors to either side, but the fenced

MICHAEL WEBB

street front and garden facade are fully glazed. Trees shade the windows in summer; in winter, with the blinds raised, the glass absorbs the low rays and cuts heating bills. Like the Eames's house, Hovey's is enriched by the reflections and shadows of mature trees, but the spirit of this house is crisper and more direct; more engineering than art, less poetry but more versatility.

The stairs spring up through a double-height volume, but a tight-planned complex of bedrooms and family rooms occupies most of the upper story. In contrast, the ground floor has few divisions. Space flows freely around the central service core. Red joists, blue stairs, and yellow accent walls enliven the space on dull days. The greatest surprise is Hovey's extraordinary collection of furniture handcrafted by the late George Nakashima. Chairs and tables, stools, settles, and a sybaritic chaise all exploit the natural irregularities of different woods, which Nakashima personally selected. Most are set off by Mies classics, and the juxtaposition of organic and machine-made, like the leaves playing against the steel frame, is what gives this house its special distinction. ∎

A steel canopy links the rear of the house to the garage, partly enclosing the yard.

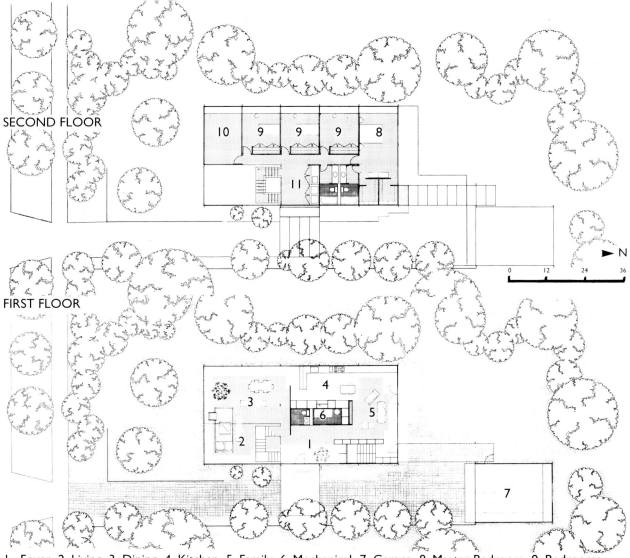

SECOND FLOOR

FIRST FLOOR

1. Foyer 2. Living 3. Dining 4. Kitchen 5. Family 6. Mechanical 7. Garage 8. Master Bedroom 9. Bedrooms
10. Playroom 11. Den

Opposite: Red joists, blue stairs, and yellow walls enliven the interior.

Below: A handcrafted settle by George Nakashima beside a classic Mies van der Rohe chair.

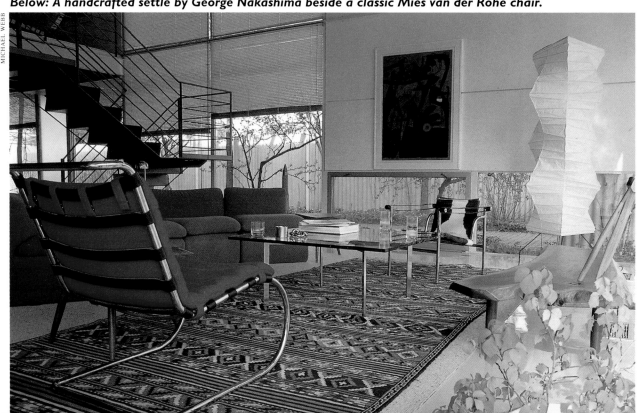

Austin, Texas, 1988–89

"I LOVE OLD HOUSES but could never find one that worked for me," says Lawrence Speck. "As a single father I had taken my two sons on a trip through Germany, and they adored the castles. And I've always admired timeless, rock-solid buildings that are open and filled with light—like the houses of [Mexican architect] Luis Barragan." So he built a light-filled castle on a leafy street, conveniently close to his flourishing practice and to the University of Texas School of Architecture where he is the dean.

By local standards the lot was small (75 x 90 feet) and there were mandatory set-backs, so Speck pushed the house as far from the street as he could and fenced the front yard. Several generations of German immigrants had used the locally abundant soft limestone for rustic masonry, so Speck had a building tradition to draw on and knew which quarry could supply the big irregular blocks he needed. "I could have got away with thinner, smaller stones, but I went for blocks that would suggest age and tolerate unskilled mortaring," he remarks. He combined the living areas in a lofty hall with 18-inch-thick walls and assymetrical windows, topped by a pitched metal roof with a wide overhang, which is laterally braced at the pitch and beneath the eaves.

In sharp contrast is the interlocking bedroom wing, concealed from the street by an open, flat-roofed carport, which doubles as a porch for play and entertaining. This lightweight, wood-frame structure is clad in Pyrok—a European cement board that is usually confined to construction sites—trimmed with horizontal redwood battens. "The change in materials and scale creates the latitude to accommodate different uses—a great room and small intimate rooms," says the architect. The contrast suggests castle and shed, and recalls the juxtaposition of brick and battened plywood in Herbert Newman's house in Connecticut.

The 2,300-square-foot house is entered at the junction of the two structures. Guests turn right past the kitchen and into the lofty living-dining room. Wood stairs lead up to a room above the kitchen that overlooks the void. Speck intended it as a study-guest room, but the boys have taken it over as an observation deck. His priority was an open, raised kitchen from which he could supervise his sons and chat with dinner guests. It seems to float within the central space.

MICHAEL WEBB

The view out is unencumbered by cabinets, which are packed in beneath the broad work surfaces. The floor is paved in red Mexican porphyry, extending back to the bedrooms, which open off the entry hall.

The living room suggests the great hall in a medieval manor, a point of transition from fortified splendor to domestic comfort. Oak floor boards play off the rough stone and deep reveals. Red- and green-framed windows, small and high on the east side for privacy, expansive to the north and south, balance the light. "I had to calculate the angle of sun to demonstrate that the roof would shade the big south window from summer sun," recalls Speck. It did, and that allowed him to secure a variance on the energy code that limits the amount of glass. Moonlight streams in, unimpeded, through the high east window.

So rich are the textures, so dramatic the shifts of scale, that few would call this a minimal house. And yet, what could be more minimal than a stone hall, an undivided shell with no applied ornament. Speck has stripped away the inessential and enriched a powerful form with well-crafted cabinets and simple detailing. He has evoked the past without copying it. "This was the first time I had built for myself, and it's hard to live inside your own work," he confesses. His sons would disagree. Not every boy has the run of a private castle. ∎

© R. GREG HURSLEY

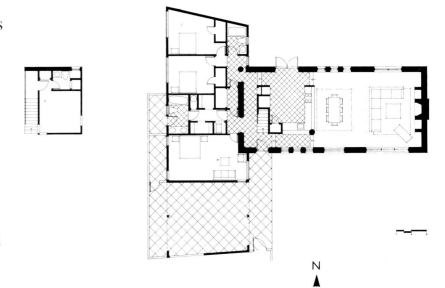

A light-filled castle with a wooden stair.

N

Rustic masonry in native limestone frames the living room and raised kitchen.

Opposite: An upstairs study-guest room commands a spectacular view of the living room.

West Stockbridge, Massachusetts, 1985–87

WESTERN MASSACHUSETTS is still Norman Rockwell country, but one of the Berkshire hills is now crowned with a house that would have baffled America's favorite illustrator. An octagon rises from a square base set into the hill. Stairs cascade from terrace to deck at front and back. Aluminium waterspouts poke out, like beaks, from the gleaming white stucco. Sharp-edged and symmetrical, the house appears grand at one minute, tiny the next.

Warren Schwartz, who practices architecture with Robert Silver in Boston, designed it as a getaway and as a second base for his wife, Sheila Fiekowsky, a violinist in the Boston Symphony, who spends her summers with the orchestra at nearby Tanglewood.

"In 1984, we spent our honeymoon in the Veneto," says Schwartz. "The most powerful villa we saw wasn't by Palladio, but by [his follower] Vincenzo Scamozzi.

Warren Schwartz, Sheila Fiekowsky, and daughter.

His Rocca Pisana at Lonigo seemed so direct and modern, and it commands the countryside around." When they returned they bought a 16-acre hillside site with great views, and began planning their house. Sheila wanted a place to make music, alone and with colleagues. She loved Chesterwood, the great cubic studio of sculptor Daniel Chester French in Stockbridge. So a well-proportioned music pavilion became a part of the program. Schwartz began sketching, but the design came slowly. "I'd get ideas during Sheila's concerts and begin drawing in the dark," he recalls. "When you build for yourself, it stirs memories. I remembered an elephant ride I took as a little kid, and the first design came out as a cubist elephant with stairs for trunk and tail and a platform on top. Then I tried something more romantic, and finally this."

Schwartz sees the 1,200-square-foot house as an abstract of images from past and future. It draws on the Rocca Pisana

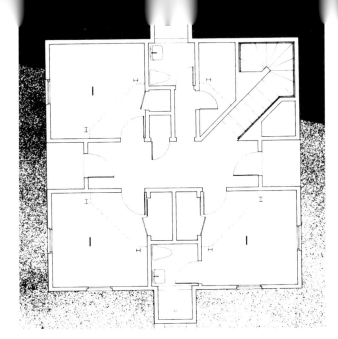

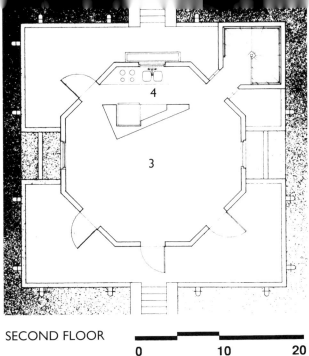

FIRST FLOOR   N ◄   SECOND FLOOR

1. Bedrooms 2. Bath 3. Conservatory 4. Kitchen

0   10   20

and the spiky forms of avant-garde buildings he had seen on the orchestra's tour of Japan. Schwartz grew up in Miami, but he wanted to avoid the pretty colors and decorative details of post-modernism, so he chose to paint it white and emphasize the fundamentals.

The base of the house is 30 feet square and contains three corner bedrooms, each a ten-foot cube. Steel columns penetrate these rooms and support the octagonal pavilion which is 20 feet high and 20 feet wide. You enter the house from doors set into the base, at either end of a corridor that bisects the invisible north-south axis of the exterior stairs, and climb a curved stair in a skylit corner tower— the one assymetrical element in the house—to the music room. This doubles as a living room, with a small kitchen concealed by a white wall, and rises to a pyramidal vault. Four sets of French windows open to the north and south terraces.

Sheila commissioned a string trio to inaugurate the house, and over 50 friends gathered around the players and on the terrace. They knew—from a favorite church in Lexington—that an octagon can provide good acoustics. The quality of sound in the house has been enhanced by the skim-coated plaster walls, maple floor, and spruce ceiling. The same woods are used in violins.

The Schwartzes now have two small children, and they spend as much time in their country retreat as the weather will allow, for the house was not designed for the harsh winters. Warren believes that "buildings should be like the people who make them, and a house should be a self- or group portrait. This was the first house I had designed in 15 years: it was an opportunity but also a great responsibility. Robert did critiques, and Sheila contributed and supported what I was doing. She was the best client I have had." ∎

The pavilion was inspired by an Italian villa and the Japanese avant-garde.
A pyramidal skylight marks the corner staircase.

Opposite: The octagonal upper room was designed for music-making.

Santa Monica, California, 1988–89

HANK KONING AND JULIE EIZENBERG were married in their native Melbourne, went to UCLA for their master's in architecture, and stayed on to establish a practice and raise a family in Santa Monica. They searched for a lot where they could realize a concept they had sketched in an earlier remodel: an extended wood-framed stucco house with interiors that would flow easily into a big garden. "We found a beautiful site, overlooking the Riviera Country Club," Hank recalls, "but it cost so much that we couldn't have afforded to build on it, so we thought of parking an Airstream trailer there and making do with nature." Instead, they bought a deep (50 x 167 foot) plot on a leafy street lined with small bungalows.

Inspired by the flounder houses of Virginia, which are built along one side of a rectangular lot and face sideways through two-story porticoes, they planned

Hank Koning and Julie Eizenberg standing beneath their vine-clad pergola.

MICHAEL WEBB

a skinny 2,400-square-foot house along the northwest boundary, opening up to a garden along the southeast. Their portico would be a simpler, one-story affair, inspired by the metal pergola of Claude Monet's house in Giverny, near Paris, and by memories of the shady verandahs of Australian homesteads which add depth to plain brick boxes. To achieve this sensible scheme, they had to battle local regulations that demanded big setbacks all around, driving each house into the center of its lot and making it impossible to orient all the rooms toward the sun. "Our previous LA house faced north—which would have been fine in Australia," comments Hank.

Their original plan was to build a single-story studio at the front of the house, but they soon discovered that the rules were written for two-story structures, so they slipped the living room in beneath the studio. That gave the front end greater importance, and they redesigned it as a solid block, cut away at the south corner, and topped with a wrap-around window recessed behind a narrow balcony and flat roof plane. They rotated this block nine degrees to the trunk of the house, opening up space for an entrance to the north, giving the whole house a sense of movement, and helping define the garden—which is closed off by a green lathe toolshed and a brick workshop. The cubic head and barrel-vaulted body of the house are linked by a glass bridge and comple-

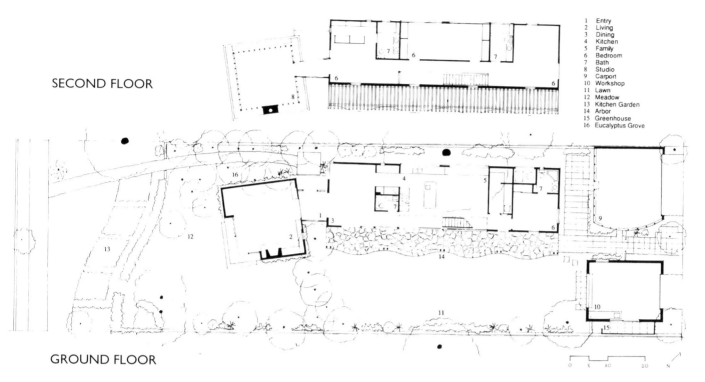

SECOND FLOOR

GROUND FLOOR

1 Entry
2 Living
3 Dining
4 Kitchen
5 Family
6 Bedroom
7 Bath
8 Studio
9 Carport
10 Workshop
11 Lawn
12 Meadow
13 Kitchen Garden
14 Arbor
15 Greenhouse
16 Eucalyptus Grove

The house has a cubic head and a barrel-vaulted body.

The bedroom corridor is cooled by ventilation flaps in the curved plywood vault.

ment each other in form, color, and function.

House and garden were planned as one. Landscape designer Bob Fletcher laid out a broad green stream that would eddy around the house and be contained by gray-green eucalyptus and guavas—species that flourish in Southern California and remind the owners of home. Rambling roses and trumpet vines now blanket the studio block, and the aluminium portico has become a green sculpture of muscat vines, shading a stone-flagged terrace with a wavy edge that was inspired by the serpentine brick walls of the University of Virginia in Charlottesville.

The ground-floor rooms open up to the garden through sliding glass doors. A free-standing guest bathroom and the pantry divide the open kitchen-family room from the dining area, but space runs as freely as do the two small boys. A steel-framed staircase leads up to a sequence of bedrooms opening off a narrow corridor beneath a smoothly curved plywood vault. Light flows down from a clerestory in the vault, and tiny ventilation flaps can be opened in summer. Slatted wooden shutters shade the corridor from direct sun.

Koning-Eizenberg stretched their tight budget by using low-cost materials in inventive ways, enhancing them with creative details. The fireplace in the living room was patterned by setting eucalyptus leaves into the wet concrete. Earth red, strong yellow, turquoise, and green brighten the stucco. The studio floor is a checkerboard of Masonite and maple-veneered plywood. Here, as in their many diversified housing projects, Koning-Eizenberg have packed a lot of ideas and useful spaces into a deceptively simple frame. But, says Julie: "You are not always concious of the design of this house. I wanted it to feel easy, and not push me around." ■

Looking from the living room through the dramatically shadowed link to the kitchen-family room.

ALFRED BROWNING PARKER (1916–)

Windsong, Coconut Grove, Florida, 1989–90

ALFRED PARKER remembers the 1926 hurricane that devastated southern Florida—his new bicycle was crushed by debris—and it taught him a lesson about building on this perilous shore. During his five decades of practice, beginning with the first of seven houses for himself, he sought to build in harmony with nature, winning praise from Frank Lloyd Wright for an organic residence that caught the master's eye. He was equally concerned with function, turning fire hoses on a new marina to check its resistance to high seas. His experience paid off when Hurricane Andrew struck, in 1992.

"Windsong" occupies the highest ground in Coconut Grove, just south of Miami, but it is protected by a palmetum, the legacy of a botanist who planted 350 different kinds of palm and a hundred other species. When Parker bought the 135-foot-square plot, the trees were so dense that they concealed everything around, and he promised the former owner that he would preserve them all or plant two for every one that was lost. His son, Quentin Dart Parker, now an architect in Los Angeles, remembers coming to the site as a small boy when his father was trying how to decide how to save the trees and provide versatile space for a large family at minimum cost. This was his fifth house, and he had learned that you can quickly outgrow a big home and get stuck with high bills for cooling space you don't need.

Three small clearings suggested separate pods, each with a primary role—living, eating and sleeping—but able to serve changing needs. Each could be cooled separately when it was in use. There was also a spring-fed well and a gravel pit on the property. Parker decided to link them with a lap pool, protected from tree debris by a covered walkway that would tie together the three pods. The 88-foot pool would spill into the pit and add its music to that of the birds. To protect the pods from termites and rot, he supported all three buildings on slabs and four-and-a-half-foot columns of poured concrete and channeled the pool above ground so that it could be cantilevered above the pit. The height limit was 32 feet, and the sleeping pod required three stories, which had to be squeezed into the 27 feet above the slab; the other two pods have one main floor and an open gallery for a total of 4,000 square feet. Sliding glass doors open onto the walkway and a dining terrace; a sauna and a cabana

MICHAEL WEBB

looking into the pool are tucked in beneath the bedrooms.

"Architecture is about the enclosure of space for utility, beauty, and durability," says Parker. "It has more to do with building than drawing and with the gut desire to create things. I built this house myself with an old laborer and a Swedish carpenter, the best way I knew how." They reused the plywood concrete forms for the walls, creating a well-insulated sandwich of plywood, plaster, and galvanized metal lath, cladding them inside and out with milled Honduras mahogany. Taking his cue from the palms, the architect rounded the corners of the pods and bleached the exterior boards to create a pale, rot-proof surface that required no further maintenance. He had the boards milled irregularly and carefully arranged them, one by one, to suggest the patterns of the palm fronds, before realizing that the effect would be just as good if he nailed them up at random.

The interiors are plain and simply furnished, with open stairs and uplights that dramatize the harmonious volumes. Tempered glass windows are hooded to shelter them from wind and rain; the master bedroom has the added protection of sliding shutters. Throughout there is a delight in fine carpentry and well-crafted efficiency.

Quentin Parker remembers the pleasure of waking to the sound of monkeys tapping on his bedroom window, as

Large expanses of glass flood the interior with light. Hoods and shutters protect windows from storms.

though he were in a terrarium and the animals were the spectators. Herons perch on the treetops, and wildlife flourishes at every level of this man-made jungle. Andrew thinned the trees, but the palmetum will recover. Meanwhile, with the children grown, Albert Parker and his wife, Frosso, have gone to live in the second of two houses he built in Vermont. How can he bear to leave the paradise he created here? "I was born in Boston, the skiing is great—and I'm sure to be back," he responds, with the energy of a man half his age. ∎

115

SECOND LEVEL

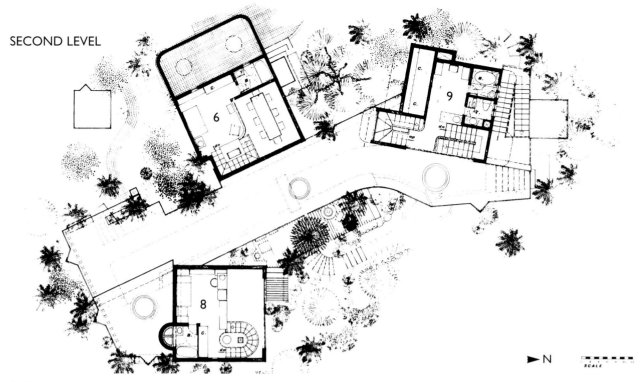

1. Entry 2. Swimming 3. Living 4. Kitchen 5. Dining 6. Bedroom 7. Pit 8. Study/Bedroom 9. Dressing

PRIMARY LEVEL

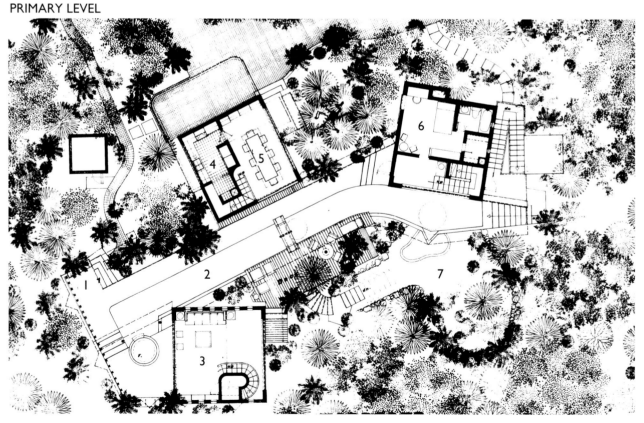

Opposite: Each of the pavilions is clad with milled and bleached Honduras mahogany.
Overleaf: A covered walkway and lap pool link three wooden pavilions. (© 1980 BO PARKER)

South Miami, Florida, 1986–87

RONEY MATEU built his first house for himself and his wife, Junie, on a busy corner to show the public what he could do. "People knocked on the door, I got work, but we couldn't afford to live there and had to sell it after six months," he recalls. He built a smaller house and then, after seven years of varied practice, a third to accommodate his two growing children and his parents, who had brought him here from Cuba in 1960. "It was a way of thanking them for their inspiring example of hard work," he explains. "They carried only $18 when they fled, and they never had a house of their own. We live in a society that packages its elders. I believe it's important to hold a family together—the kids and their grandparents need each other."

Mateu designed and built two houses which face each other across a pool and walled garden from either end of a 80 x 300-foot corner lot. For himself he created a crisply stuccoed concrete block and glass box that dramatizes its two-story volume; for his parents, a traditionally planned bungalow, with smaller windows and a pitched roof. They conduct a dialogue of the generations across an outdoor living room which everyone shares—a symbol of community and a way of living. The pool is a reminder of the water that separates them from their homeland; the colonnade pulls them close.

Miami was developed by northerners, many of whom sought escape from its steamy heat within solid walls and air-conditioned cocoons. The newly arrived Cubans felt entirely at home, and this helps explain the success many of them have had in designing stylish hot-weather houses, infusing traditional models with a new sophistication. Mateu has taken a different route from many of his fellow emigres. "This is a classic modern house that assembles ordinary elements in an extraordinary way," he explains, "and it was driven by creative economies and by a response to the climate. We wanted the interior to feel naturally light and cool. Virtually everything in the house, except the furniture, was bought off the shelf."

A module of two feet high and three feet four inches wide establishes the scale. The 2,700-square-foot house has few openings to the street, to protect against noise and sun from the south and west. A lofty corrugated fiberglass-vaulted

Opposite: A two-story screen porch serves as an intermediary room between house and courtyard.

GROUND LEVEL

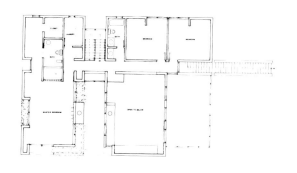

SECOND LEVEL

atrium serves as a covered entrance court, establishes a bold axis through the open staircase, and separates house from carport and workroom. Mateu adores cars and would have preferred a roll-up garage door at the entrance and a concrete floor throughout, making the house an extension of the garage, but Junie vetoed that idea. Instead he chose a tile that is as close to concrete as he could get. Concrete garden paths were sprinkled with rock salt before they set; later this was hosed off to leave a texture like that of coral rock.

The entry hall is a crossroads, bisected by a cross axis that extends out through the steps that lead up to the roof terrace. Each axis frames a view of trees and sky, enhancing the openness, transparency, and cross-ventilation of the house. The dining-kitchen areas are linked by Mateu's jagged marble table and breakfast counter, and set off by a wall clad in corrugated steel. They flow into the 20-foot-high living room, a dramatic white void animated by barred shadows. Fans turn lazily overhead. A low window to the south reveals the terra-cotta garden wall and a bed of flowers; high windows to the west frame tree tops. Across the east side are glass doors that open into a

double-height screen porch, which serves as a buffer zone between house and garden. Its aluminium grid ties the house together and the dark mesh cuts the sun's heat and glare.

A study is incorporated into the master bedroom and there is no family room. "We spend most of the time outdoors, year-round—why build something you don't need," says Mateu. "A house should be a backdrop for the people who live in it, anonymous and flexible enough for other people—even if they furnish it with antiques. Luis Barragan showed how simple things can look beautiful beneath a tropical sun, and that helped me impose limits on my invention." ■

Opposite: The living room, looking south through the low window that frames the garden.

Below: A lofty fiberglass-vaulted atrium serves as a covered entrance court.

Hillsborough, California, 1986–90

THE OU HOUSE is named for Joy's parents who, like Cornelius Van der Leeuw providing a loan to Richard Neutra, made it possible for the husband-wife partnership of Tim Kobe and Joy Ou to design a house for their family and to share it with three generations of her's. Jong Fa and Chen Ching Ou raised Joy in Taiwan, but she took her degree in environmental design at the Art Center College of Design in Pasadena, where she met Tim Kobe. Working together as Kobeou Associates, they try to combine the best of both cultures in their large-scale projects around the Pacific Rim.

"We were interested in how to pool resources to create a richer, more versatile place and give everyone a sense of community," says Tim. "These were ideas we had explored in a housing competition. It's much harder to design just for your-

self, because of the intimacy and emotional involvement. Here we had to ask: 'What qualities of space, what patterns of living are most meaningful for ourselves and others?'"

The parents trusted the architects to meet their specific needs, but intitially proposed that there be a room for everyone in the family—19 people in all. Since it was unlikely that this busy, scattered family would assemble more than once a year, Tim suggested that nine bedrooms might be enough. They found an idyllic hilltop site, part of a former estate with a view east over San Francisco Bay, half an hour south of the city. Their plan was to split the traditional Chinese courtyard house into two opposed U shapes, flanking an entry hall and partly enclosing patios. The front patio would be used for family activities; the one in back for outdoor entertaining. By dividing the two-story house in this way, the architects managed to preserve nearly all the mature trees and reduce the bulk of the 11,000-square-foot house—at the price of increased heating bills.

Architects on the local design review board approved the plans; other members objected on grounds of size, but also with lightly veiled hints that their exclusive community would be overrun by Chinese. The architects persuaded some sceptics by showing them a scale model on the site. Eventually their plans benefited from the hostility. Design review boards often

LOU LABONTE

The dining room fuses traditional Chinese and contemporary California taste.

tinker with more conventional proposals; this became an either-or issue, and the board finally granted approval without conditions. Once the house was built, it and its owners were readily accepted, but the ordeal left an unpleasant memory.

The wood-framed house with steel-reinforced cantilevers is clad in color-flecked stucco, which picks up on the colors of moss and rocks to give the structure a rooted quality, alternating with concrete block walls. Trees screen the house in summer. A path leads from the garage to an impassive facade that conceals the view beyond. You enter the square entry hall and discover that the staircase and cross-axial corridors are set at odd angles. Tim explains that his parents-in-law firmly believe in the

principles of *feng shui*, which have governed Chinese (and Japanese) planning since time immemorial. Devised by priests, who may have been the first architects, they began as common-sense rules to keep buildings safe and healthy but later became an arcane set of superstitions. Doors, passages, and stairs must be set at angles to each other so that good spirits cannot fly out and bad spirits are checked at the threshold. Kobeou turned these constraints to advantage, using the shifts to create a dynamic relationship between the spaces and to point the staircase toward Mount Diablo.

The subtleties of this bold but minimal house elude most photos. The mix of rough and refined materials animates the big volumes. Exposed concrete block

SECOND FLOOR

FIRST FLOOR

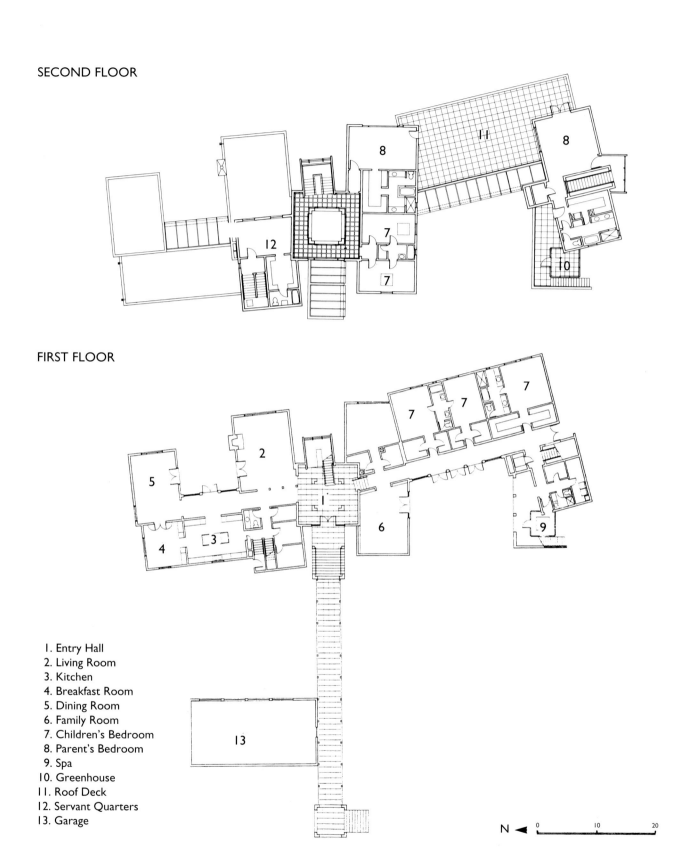

1. Entry Hall
2. Living Room
3. Kitchen
4. Breakfast Room
5. Dining Room
6. Family Room
7. Children's Bedroom
8. Parent's Bedroom
9. Spa
10. Greenhouse
11. Roof Deck
12. Servant Quarters
13. Garage

N

Looking across one of the two open-sided patios to the "Buddha tower."

walls—polished on the inside—complement bird's-eye maple floors, fine cabinetry, and an eclectic mix of Asian and American craft furniture. The main staircase is treated as a sculpture, its canted risers zig-zagging up between acid-washed copper walls. Open doors frame windows, windows frame trees and distant views or slide past floors and decks to link two stories. The house has a hierarchy of scale and formality that adjusts to every activity and number.

The grandparents have a second-floor apartment that opens onto a shared deck, a two-story hothouse for Mr. Ou's orchids, and a tower with a glass bay, from which Mrs. Ou can invoke the blessings of the Buddha on her household. Tim and Joy loved their former house in the city and had planned to remodel it and move back after a few years. But now, they look forward to escaping the summer fogs and relaxing with the good spirits on the hill. ■

© CHRISTOPHER IRION

Above: Corridors, staircase, and entry hall are set at odd angles to each other.

Opposite: Rough and refined textures in a skylit corridor that opens the house to the outdoors.

ARQUITECTONICA has done more than any architectural firm since Morris Lapidus to redefine the public image of Miami. The pink stucco, glass-brick Spear House (built for Laurinda's parents), and the Atlantis condominium block, with its punched out sky deck, were beamed around the world as visual leitmotifs of "Miami Vice." More exuberant offices,

shopping centers, and houses followed, from Lima to Los Angeles. But the husband-wife partners who had created these traffic-stoppers decided to do it differently for themselves and their six small children.

"We wanted it to be low key—my parents always had problems with sight-seers—but even here people find us," says Laurinda Spear, who is a native of Miami. "It was inspired by the house we were living in, which was very Floridian, with the small windows they had in 1900.

We didn't want high tech, or a great expanse of glass." Bernardo Fort-Brescia, who was born in Peru, concurs: "This is a compact, modest house for a family of eight, with no grand ceremonial spaces. All the rooms are used by the whole family. It's tall and rectangular, to free up most of the site for play, and it's painted gray-green so that it disappears into the trees."

Like a small child covering her eyes and believing herself to be invisible, the house stands out despite its reticence— even more since Hurricane Andrew stripped away many of the trees. But it is easier now to appreciate the skill with which the architects have articulated a plain three-story 4,300-square-foot house, creating a diagonal checkerboard of windows that wrap around corners, poke out as bays, and sprout white "eyebrows" like the streamline moderne apartments in South Miami Beach. There, the protrusions are consistent in form and intended merely to animate plain surfaces; here they are curved and triangular and play a double role—to protect open windows from tropical showers and cast changing shadows across the facades. Service rooms line the south front of the top floor—for privacy and protection from the sun—and window openings are partly blocked with blue tiles. The bedroom windows on the other sides are varied— one has a balcony, another has shutters, a third has a bay—to give each its unique

SECOND FLOOR

FIRST FLOOR

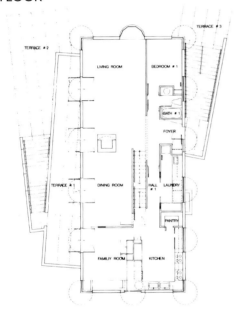

GROUND FLOOR

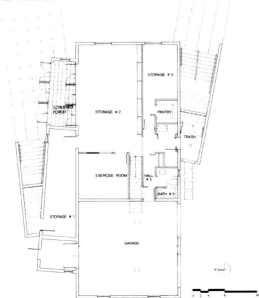

character. Quartzite steps leading to the mid-level entrance are set at an angle to the block.

Visitors can expect to be checked out by a succession of small figures peering through the etched fishes in the glass of the front door, which adds to the sense that you are in a magic place, a little removed from the real world. The interior could not be simpler. "Bernardo would have made it entirely open," says Laurinda. "I wanted a separate dining room, sealed off like a compartment in a submarine." In fact, space flows freely around a central core of stairs, though doors can be closed to achieve privacy for a dinner party. Floors are of bleached oak, the fireplace is of shellstone, and the stair rail is of handcrafted cypress. The walls are hung with an eclectic mix of maps, historic prints, and folk art. Furniture is equally diverse: a red sheet-metal chair by Howard Meister, a late-18th-century sofa, hand-me-downs, and modern

Overleaf: The house is designed to fit unobtrusively into its leafy surroundings. (MICHAEL WEBB)

Below: White "eyebrows" protect windows from tropical showers.

MICHAEL WEBB

Space flows freely around the hearth and a central stair core.

rarities. The corner kitchen is Mission Central, with views through the house, up and down stairs. The playroom below opens into the garden.

The interior is so tight-knit that it's almost impossible to capture in photos the subtle layering of spaces and the harmony of proportions, which prove, if proof were needed, that Arquitectonica can do serious architecture as well as commercial spectaculars. Here their fires are banked down, and function comes well ahead of form. Says Laurinda in mock despair, "Small children are like a wolf pack that wants to huddle with its parents in one bathroom and one bedroom. It was a waste designing so many." But she and Bernardo are looking forward to their next house, which will be on an island where they will have the chance to be "a little more daring." ■

Toronto, Canada, 1991–92

IN THE LEAFY ENCLAVE OF ROSEDALE, a
few miles from the bustling core of
Canada's largest city, Donald McKay has
designed a 6,400-square-foot urban loft
that is tough and refined, spacious yet
intimate; a place for family life and entertaining, art and study. A muscular, red
steel structural frame penetrates and supports a brick-walled block, which protects
the art from direct light and offers a snug
retreat from harsh winters. The frame
extends out to support lightweight glass
and aluminium curtain walls that wrap
around three sides of the core like a high-
tech screen porch, enclosing airy, sun-
filled volumes and extending the house
into the landscape. Massive free-standing
steel canopies at front and back double as
porches and sculpture.

For McKay the house is a bridge
between the city and its first garden sub-
urb—his contribution to the harmonious
diversity of North America's most livable
metropolis. And it reflects the range of
his interests, from furniture and interior
design to architecture and urban planning,
all of which he teaches, writes about, and
practices in his offices downtown. His
wife, Sandra Simpson, is a respected
dealer in conceptual art, some of which
is on display, and they have a small
daughter.

They found the site occupied by a
classic modern house and garden that had
deteriorated beyond recovery and had to
be cleared. The street is lined with an
eclectic mix of traditional houses.
Happily, most Canadians do not share the
fierce intolerance of the unfamiliar so
common in many U.S. communities, so
McKay had a fairly free hand. But he was
careful to respect the scale and setbacks
of his neighbors and to use warm brick to
soften the impact at the front. He
describes his approach to the design as
"building up layers of diagrams until they
thicken, to achieve a series of overlapping
layers. The house is about boxes, an

SIMON POSEN

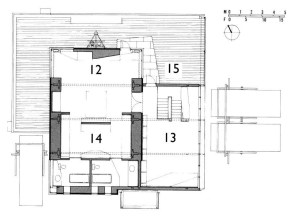

THIRD FLOOR

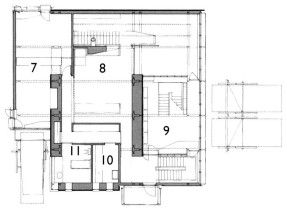

SECOND FLOOR

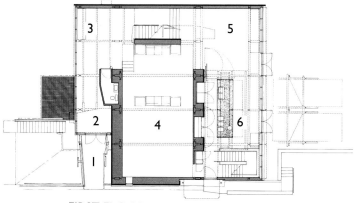

FIRST FLOOR

1. Bridge 2. Entry Vestibule 3. Closet Unit
4. Living/Entertaining 5. Dining Space 6. Kitchen
7. Bedroom 8. Living Room 9. Lower Library
10. Laundry 11. Bathroom 12. Master Bedroom
13. Upper Library 14. Dressing Room 15. Roof Deck

opportunity to find fresh solutions." A low-ceilinged kitchen and living room complement the lofty dining area, which opens onto the garden in fine weather. Upstairs, suspended within this outer volume, is a two-story library leading out onto a roof deck. Sitting room and master bedroom are stacked above the living room in the core.

Industrial lofts, the Eames house, and the integration of structure and ornament in the work of Gottfried Semper, architect of the Dresden Opera, all contributed ideas to this richly textured complex. McKay designed the structural steel frame, with help from Peter Sheffield, and it was erected in two days—the porches in four hours—from pre-assembled units that were welded together on site. Within, it is as ubiquitous as Pierre Charreau's classic Glass House (1933) in Paris. Beams rise through the white oak floors and extend through walls, fly though space, frame cabinets, and support the aluminium grid that screens the wall-to-wall glazing on the garden front. Elegantly detailed sections emerge beside the bathroom and study windows, providing cozy nooks for cats to snooze in.

In this peaceable kingdom, industrial and craft elements lie down together. The steel drawbridge and portcullis-like canopy over the entry have a tough stance

Opposite: Cabinets are attached to the structural steel frame.

The steel, brick, and aluminum street facade respects the scale of its traditional neighbors.

The house and sculptural steel canopies open up to the garden.

that is subverted by the delicacy of interior details and the softly filtered light. McKay's tables—a smooth wooden boomerang on a spiky wheeled base, an elegantly cut and folded steel plate—share space with comfortable sofas and mission chairs. The steel and wood staircase is a masterly sculpture, as are the gull-wing wood screens that fold down over the kitchen island, transforming working space into a sleek area for entertaining. The architect even commissioned Fruehauf, the truck manufacturer, to develop an improved aluminium-coated cladding panel.

"I think of the house as an inventor's workshop, a place to try things out, just as I do when I am designing furniture," says McKay. "I like to erode corners, to blur boundaries between different functions, and to use the stairs as enormous pieces of furniture to bridge different zones. What has surprised me the most is the tremendous range of light and shadow and the way the sun sets through the house." ■

The sun-filled kitchen and dining room face south over the garden.

Albuquerque, New Mexico, 1983–84; 1990

ELEVEN YEARS AGO, Bart Prince designed a three-story house-studio—though he had a small practice and little money—and took his plans to the building office. Someone said, "He's never going to put this up, give him a permit!" Working with a few student helpers, Prince built it himself—on a narrow corner lot surrounded by mature trees and tiny adobe cottages. "I was surprised by how much attention it got," he says. "One man looked over his shoulder as he passed and impaled his car on a fire hydrant." His neighbors didn't object, but the few people who did were among those who complained, six years later, when he began adding a tower. "This is a landmark," they protested. He replied, "It's still my house!"

Prince is a maverick, in line of succession to Wright, Bruce Goff (1904–82), and other fiercely independent mid-Westerners who pursued their visions of an organic architecture growing from the land in defiance of Eastern critics. A protege of Goff during his last decade, Prince

Bart Prince on the balcony of his house-studio.

did the working drawings for and supervised construction of Goff's last major project—the Shin'enkan Pavilion of Japanese Art in Los Angeles. In the same year he stepped into his master's shoes, he secured a loan to purchase his home site. A year later he paid it off and began building.

"I had previously designed a few houses, but this was my most ambitious," he recalls. "I didn't have the money when I started, and I couldn't get a loan. If I had thought it out, I might not have done it. I wanted it to be a sculptural expression of a place to live and work." Asked why it took the form it did, he quotes Picasso: "If I could explain it in words, I wouldn't need to paint."

The 4,500-square-foot house-studio suggests a counter-culture space colony, bafflingly intricate in detail, but quite logical in its basic design. At the noisier east end is a circular drafting office, to the west is a smaller circular studio-living area. Brick ramps wind down to these sunken areas. Four steel columns, enclosed in wood-framed, tile-clad concrete cylinders, support an upper story of bedrooms, bathroom, and den above an open deck. Stairs wind up through two of the cylinders; bathrooms and services occupy the other two. Steel pipes support the fanned, sawtooth roof over the studio, wrap around the upper story, and project out like antennae to carry canvas awnings.

GROUND FLOOR   THIRD FLOOR

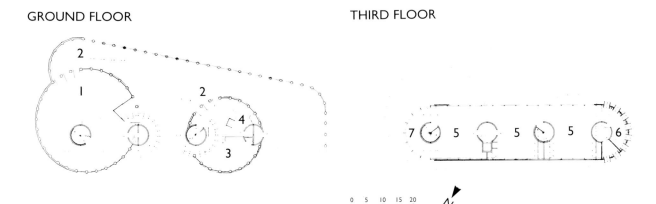

1. Studio 2. Patio 3. Living 4. Kitchen 5. Bedrooms 6. Bathroom 7. Deck

0 5 10 15 20

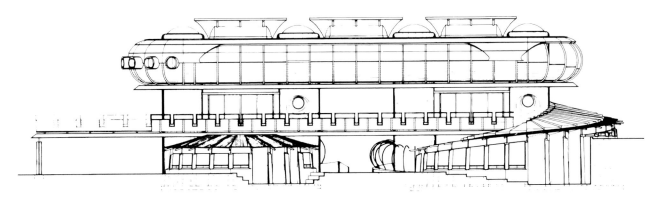

Tile-clad concrete cylinders raise the private areas a story above the ground-floor studio. (© ALAN WEINTRAUB)

Throughout, the house is a laboratory of inexpensive materials, ingeniously used: tile to reflect light, cork for bulletin boards and to absorb sound, white shag carpet running up the walls (a favorite device of Goff's). Plastic cylinders of water serve as passive solar collectors along the south side of the office and living areas. "The building had to be loose enough to allow for imperfections," says Prince. "I couldn't afford to rip them out, but I'd have been in trouble if I'd had a lot of money."

Prince strove for lightness, a feeling that the building "was being held down rather than held up," using the open deck to lighten the mass. He set it back from its smaller neighbors, burrowed into the ground and built high to bridge earth and sky and relate to the scale of the wide street intersection and big trees. In recent years, the office has been expanded, a plastic canopy has been replaced by perforated metal, and additional studio space has been enclosed on the intermediate deck, compromising its openness.

The tapered concrete-block tower was added in 1990. Monumental and fireproof, it houses rare books and archives at the base, storage and utilities at the two upper levels. Bridges cantilever out to within an inch of the south front. Its solid, vertical thrust is the perfect complement to the light horizontal structure. Water cascades down a side channel to mute traffic noise, and a flight of open steps winds around the upper story to give access to the roof.

Over the past decade, Prince has built ever grander houses, for people who can afford anything but are seduced by his unique vision. The seed was planted here. But, he says, "I wasn't looking for a place to impress potential clients. This house has probably lost me jobs. Some clients have seen it and said, 'We don't want anything like this!' I reply: 'I don't see why you should. I did this for myself.'" ■

Overleaf: Studio at east end. (© ALAN WEINTRAUB)

Opposite: White shag carpet covers walls and floor on the top floor; plastic water cylinders serve as solar collectors. (© ALAN WEINTRAUB)

Below: Breakfast counter in the living area.

Waccabuc, New York, 1967–70

MYRON GOLDFINGER grew up in a cramped apartment in Atlantic City, dreaming of "building the houses I never lived in." He studied architecture at the University of Pennsylvania, where Louis Kahn inspired him to reach beyond the commonplace. And he made a seven-year odyssey around the Mediterranean, following in the footsteps of Le Corbusier, exploring the organic architecture of North Africa, the Greek islands, the south of Italy, and Spain. He described the impact it had on him: "Building blocks. Simple structure. Clarity of purpose. And what striking forms. What power. What sculpture." The experience generated a book, *Villages in the Sun* (1969; republished in 1993), and a philosophy for his own practice.

In that book appears a sketch of "a prototype for a vacation village...a system of prefabricated wood boxes of a 15-by-15-foot modular grid with generous balconies and connecting bridges." Prefabrication was in the air; Habitat in Montreal was also intended as a prototype for industrialized building. Little came of this flurry of interest. The resort was never built, but the design became—after a two-year struggle—a house for himself and his wife, June, on ten acres of woodland. Why so much land when he had almost no money? Goldfinger explains: "The landowner saw what I had proposed and insisted I buy the properties on either side of the one I wanted because, he said, 'No-one will want to live next to you!' And the Waccabuc design review board was shocked because it wasn't fake colonial."

The concept came in a flash, though it may have germinated during the years of his travels. He chose the 15-foot module as a comfortable size for the major rooms and created a four-story structure that spirals up from four blocks at the base to one at the top, with decks cantilevered out and inward. "Each pitched roof is at right angles to the next, which fuses the structure externally and creates a sweeping interlocking series of vertical spaces within," he explains. A three-story studio is linked to the house by a second-story bridge. It is a distillation of Kahn and the kasbah, of forms that were born in the strong clear light of the Mediterranean.

But Goldfinger is a city boy who wanted to live in the woods. The house is faced with the same weathered cedar boards as neighboring farms and is rooted in granite outcrops. On a stormy day it is less sculptural object than mysterious

June and Myron Goldfinger.

The modular wooden house was inspired by traditional Mediterranean buildings.

presence. He calls it Tyranosaurus Rex and has thoughtfully provided a dark rock pool at which the dragon can drink (it doubles as a Jacuzzi for humans). June likens the house to the fantasies kids have before they start living by other people's expectations, calling it "a habitable sculpture, and a great foil to the environment. The Indians would love it."

The entry is enigmatic—across granite boulders, through a sliding glass door in a blank wall, and around another wall to the mud room that doubles as wine cellar and a stash for Goldfinger's eclectic hoard. There is a vintage high chair from Texas, an Irish breakfast table, a Rastafarian bird cage, and a Magnolia Oil sign. A right turn takes you into an alcove with a Corbusier chaise and a close-up of the woods; a left turn leads into the living-dining room. The house, so pristine in the early photographs, now contains a rich trove of objects—a model train set has invaded the laundry—and an eclectic

choice of modern furniture, including several classics from the late lamented Design Research store.

The second-floor kitchen has no window—the architect thought it a pity to break the sheer expanse of the entrance wall. The third-floor master bedroom, relocated in what used to be the studio, has a canted skylight and mirrors to either side that give the tiny space a sense of infinity. The daughters have grown and left their sleeping galleries; Goldfinger has expanded the house inward, glassing over two of the decks—for an extension of the master bedroom and a cactus garden that reminds the owners of the desert.

In his 25 years of practice, Goldfinger has created a succession of grand geometric volumes, all of which build on his first love for the Mediterranean vernacular. But, he confesses, "I could not have built this house for any of the clients I have had over the years." ∎

FOURTH FLOOR

SECOND FLOOR

BEDROOM

DECK

DECK

STUDIO

DECK

BRIDGE

DINING
ROOM

KITCHEN

LIVING
ROOM

DECK

FOYER

DECK

BEDROOM

0 5 10 15

N
▲

THIRD FLOOR

FIRST FLOOR

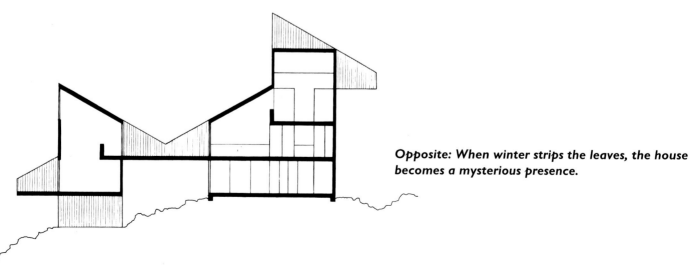

*Opposite: When winter strips the leaves, the house
becomes a mysterious presence.*

A terrace was enclosed to create a desert garden.

Plain interiors set off the owners' eclectic hoard.

Chicago, Illinois, 1970–72

AS A PARTNER in the Chicago office of Skidmore, Owings & Merrill, Walter Netsch was chief designer on two of the most ambitious and controversial projects of the 1960s: the Air Force Academy in Colorado Springs and the Chicago Campus of the University of Illinois. In the wake of those intimidatingly vast and rigorous projects, Netsch developed his "field theory" of overlaid, rotated squares on a modest scale in his house and other small projects. Here the geometric principles go beyond pattern-making to achieve a satisfying intricacy, humanizing the austere rectilinearity of Mies and other modern pioneers.

"I was traveling around the world at that time, so my first idea was an apartment for my wife, Dawn, [a state senator, now state controller]," says Netsch. "Then I decided to build a house as a 40-foot cube on an empty 40 x 75-foot lot in Old Town." Today, it is a desirable location; in the late 1960s this was the kind of decaying neighborhood that was being levelled in the name of urban renewal.

"I was being beaten up as a modernist by the first generation of post-modernists," Netsch recalls, "so I was determined that this house would show them what I could do. It was influenced by my work on the Air Force chapel; a ceremonial parade through an open, geometric volume with light streaming through." He carried around sketches of rotated squares for two years, struggling

to satisfy the intellectual and practical demands, until one day when it all came together at Dulles Airport while he was waiting between flights.

You could walk past the house without noticing it. A sheer wall of handsome brown brick, softened by a screen of trees and flowers, wraps around a corner, deferring to the scale and building lines of its neighbors. The reticent facade makes the interior seem even more dramatic. From the corner entry, your eye is drawn up and forward through a dynamically angled, multi-levelled volume that is lit from above and from a tiny enclosed courtyard. Within the cube of white concrete blocks, every wall and stair is set at an angle, leading down to an enclosed guest bedroom and study, and up to a succession of open, unrailed platforms. The geometry of the roof, roughly made of the same flitch beams that farmers use,

A sheer wall of brown brick screened by bushes.

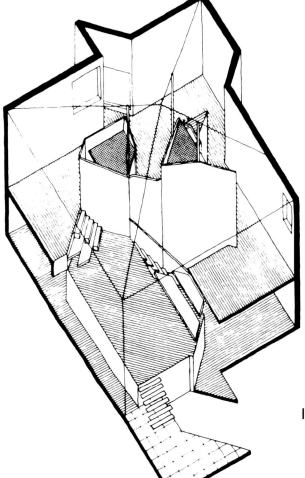

Opposite: The reticent facade makes the interior seem even more dramatic than it is.

152

The geometry of the flitch beam roof mirrors the plan of the house.

mirrors the plan of the house, in which the planes reach toward the corners.

Netsch describes the house as a laboratory, built at minimal cost from standard parts. A critic likened it to a theater, with stages at different levels and walls as wings, and it plays that role well when a hundred people gather for one of his wife's fund raisers and the stairs serve as bleachers. The bare walls provide a gallery for canvases by Robert Motherwell and Roy Lichtenstein, Gene Davis, and Ellsworth Kelly, and constructions by Donald Judd and John Okulich, which Netsch bought before these artists achieved their present fame. A clutter of furniture, rugs, and plants provides a

sense of warmth and intimacy and softens the geometry.

Dining, kitchen, and master bedroom suite are all on one level, and now that Netsch is no longer as agile as he was, he enjoys the convenience of this compact "apartment" within the void. Kids love running up the stairs and climbing to the top of towers that house bathroom and closets. Netsch retired from Skidmore, Owings & Merrill 15 years ago, but he is still designing new projects and improving a gazebo above the garage, from which he can enjoy the gingko tree he planted in the courtyard when the house was new. ■

RAYMOND KAPPE (1927–)

Pacific Palisades, California, 1965–67

RAYMOND KAPPE built about 70 post and beam structures in his first 15 years of practice, mostly small wooden houses, then made a big leap in scale to build his own in the aptly named Rustic Canyon in west Los Angeles. Massive laminated beams span six hollow concrete towers which support the sweeping planes of the house above a 45 degree slope, with a spring trickling beneath. Critic Charles Jencks called it "Mies in wood"; you could also compare it to Wright's Fallingwater.

Both masters inspired Kappe, as did Eric Mendelsohn, the German modernist who taught at Berkeley when Kappe was there. But he sees himself as an heir to Harwell Harris and the woodsy tradition of 20th-century California architecture that began with Greene and Greene. "I could have built it in steel—there would have been very little difference in cost," he says. "If I had, it might have changed my career. After this, all my clients wanted wood, even where I would have preferred to use steel. The houses I'm

Raymond Kappe on the living room deck; dining area and raised kitchen to the right.

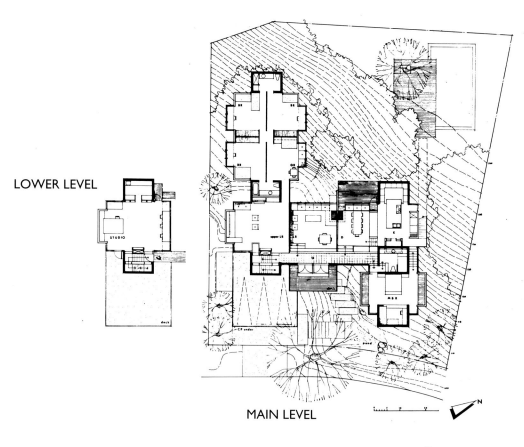

LOWER LEVEL

MAIN LEVEL

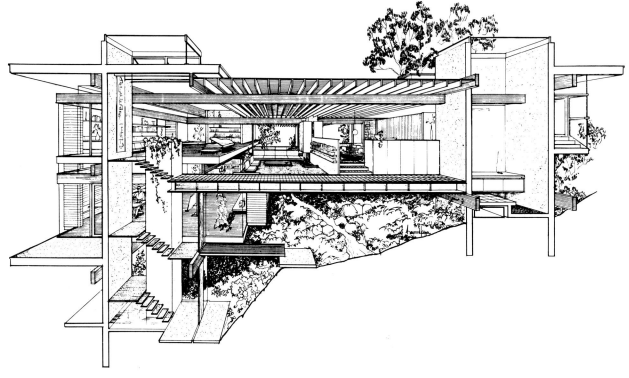

156

doing today are all related to this one."

"It was designed in three weeks because I had secured a building permit and had to start before it expired," he recalls. "The plan was simple: parents in one corner, my three kids in the opposite corner, living space [on different levels] between, and an all-purpose sunken studio." It wasn't quite as simple as he makes it sound. He began excavation for a more conventional design but discovered that the ground was so waterlogged that building there would pose the risk of sliding into the street, as a neighboring site had. He supported the house on concrete pads up to 50 feet apart, cantilevering the beams beyond the towers.

Thus, almost by chance, arose one of the seminal modern houses of Los Angeles. It is a post and beam structure, simple but grand; very Japanese in its horizontality, in its use of redwood beams, and its integration with the densely planted hillside. You climb steps from the street beneath a massive projecting deck that shelters the carport. You enter at the threshold of the studio and climb some more steps that seem to be carved from a solid block of wood, unrailed but reassuringly solid. From the upper living room you look across a depressed sitting area at the center to the dining room and, a little above, the kitchen. It reads almost as clearly as the cutaway section, but as you move through you discover how rich an experience it offers.

There is a feeling of calm in this timeless, harmoniously proportioned interior. But your eye is drawn to the dramatic vistas: north-south along the slope; east-west from street to garden. Light from the clerestories at the sides balances that from the expansive windows at front and back. Reflections add depth to the 4,000 square feet of open space and you feel as though you are expanding to fill it.

Other things you discover, walking through, include a skylit breakfast nook and a staircase, each enclosed within one of the towers. The master bedroom has a sunken toplit hearth, giving it the character of a sybaritic shrine. Steps lead from the rear to an upper garden and pool and back to a roof deck.

Kappe has built many other important houses since this, and in 1972 he became the founding director of SCI-ARC (the Southern California Institute of Architecture), which has become a spearhead of the avant-garde, and a magnet for innovative talents from around the world. But, in discussing his work, he grows nostalgic: "I didn't think of this house as a demonstration for clients. You didn't have to stand on your head to get work back then. It was cheap to build—this house cost $18 a square foot, plus $15,000 for the site. I hit it just right, time-wise." ■

157

Concrete towers and laminated beams support the sweeping planes of the house above a 45-degree slope.

View from kitchen to sunken studio. Shifts of level articulate the expansive interior.

Palm Springs, California, 1963–64; 1970

MANY CONTEMPORARY ARCHITECTS have been influenced by Le Corbusier; Albert Frey spent a formative year (1928–29) working for the great pioneer in Paris after leaving his native Zurich. Later he moved to New York, where he designed the radical Aluminaire show house, and on to Palm Springs, from where he wrote to Le Corbusier: "The California desert continues to charm me, continues to nourish me, to give me an opportunity for modern architecture, from time to time. It is a most interesting experience to live in a wild, savage, natural setting, far from the big city...." He praises the lack of regulations and continues, "The result of this freedom is that parcels of land look like laboratories of architectural and materials research....Fortunately, one only expects a house to last 30 years."

Albert Frey in his 90th year.

Sixty years later, he is still practicing in Palm Springs, and though the house he built for himself in 1940–41 recently succumbed to a fit of speculative greed, his second has achieved the 30-year mark and still looks fresh. Frey helped transform Palm Springs, building over a hundred houses, offices, schools, and hotels, as well as a hospital and city hall. After three decades of life in the flats, he moved up to what was then the highest building plot in the area—a rock bluff 220 feet above the desert floor. Like Taliesin West, the house hugs its rocky site and is almost invisible until you step up through the concrete block retaining wall to the terrace. Its lack of pretension comes as a shock after the moneyed excesses below; except for the pool, it would suggest the cave of a hermit who had turned his back on Babylon.

Frey had searched five years for a suitable eminence and then had to enlarge it with 50 loads of compacted sand to accommodate a pool-terrace. The steel-framed, rectilinear pavilion is anchored to the mountain by a granite spur around which the glass has been set. It was an inspired idea to dovetail the compact, rational structure with this romantic outcrop. The rock separates the bedroom from the living-dining room and plays the symbolic role of a hearth. Its height determined that of the roof, which has a 12 degree slope to shed winter showers. In 1970 Frey extended the house to the west,

MICHAEL WEBB

to add a guest bedroom, facing the walls with steel up to the clerestory to block the fierce afternoon sun.

Indoors, wood has been brushed with white stain and the ceiling enameled midnight blue to soften the sun's glare. Together with the rust-brown roof, sage-green walls, and the yellow and green draperies, these colors integrate the house with rocks, plants, and sky.

"When my father died, the old house was bigger than I needed," says Frey. "I wanted something minimal, that eliminated the inessential and required no maintenance. It was also an opportunity to experiment with natural air conditioning." Summer temperatures in Palm Springs can rise to 110 degrees in the shade, and there is no shade here, only rocks to radiate the heat. Frey sandwiched eight inches of fiberglass insulation between the corrugated steel roof (Cor Ten steel on the addition) and a lining of perforated, corrugated aluminium to absorb heat and sound. The overhanging roof blocks the midday sun in summer; in winter the glass serves as a passive solar collector. Inside, mirrored blinds deflect the heat and create an air pocket behind the glass. Sliding glass doors can be opened front and back to achieve cross ventilation.

The 1,130-square-foot interior is tightly planned—the product of "a Depression-era impulse to make every inch and every dollar count." In the living area, two sleep-sofas are set at an angle to each other and built into mahogany plywood storage cabinets. Steps lead up to a counter that serves as a dining and drafting table. The angle and shift of level animate the room, but what makes the house feel expansive are the panoramas of rocks, sky, and the city below. Frey admired the concept of "borrowed scenery" in Japan and, as he casually remarks, "I learned how to frame views working with Le Corbusier on the Villa Savoie." ∎

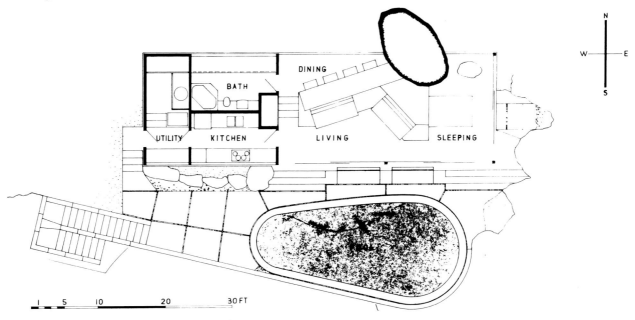

A simple shelter and pool, clinging to the mountains high above Palm Springs.

A volcanic boulder anchors the house and divides the bed from the living area.

Franklin, Michigan, 1988–89

THE 5,100-SQUARE-FOOT house that Kenneth Neumann built for his family in a historic community just north of Detroit performs a disappearing act worthy of a master magician. An expanse of glass can be glimpsed through the trees from the street below the property; a ground-hugging wall of crisp gray and white striped clapboard is all that can be seen from from the street above. The house is an elegant abstraction of the colonial vocabulary that takes its place alongside its eclectic neighbors. A community review board approved the concept. The rest of the block had no objections, but a few busybodies objected and delayed final approval. Neumann stood firm. "Most of my clients work for the auto industry and are very conservative," he observes. "I wish now that I had been more cutting-edge in designing for myself."

The site shaped the design. A client had bought the lot, hoping to create a

MICHAEL WEBB

dream house for his new bride, but found it too steep, sandy, and full of trees to build on. Neumann snapped it up and realized his dream—which included a north-facing studio for his bride, artist Beverly Neumann. He juggled the plan in order to preserve all but two of the mature trees and oriented the house to the north, so that the studio, living, and sleeping areas would overlook a spring-fed pond at the bottom of the hill through expansive, double-glazed windows and from cantilevered decks. And he stayed within the mandatory height limit of 27 feet by setting the three-story house down the slope so that the 42-foot-high rear facade was offset by the front, which rises only 10 feet above the street. That justified the flat roofs—which he preferred for their own sake—and preserved a view of the pond for his neighbors up the hill.

"I wanted an architect's house that was rational and artistic, that would make and break a grid and would emphasize the horizontal to play off the trees," says Neumann. An admirer of Louis Kahn, who liked to express the separateness of "servant" and "served" spaces, he concentrated the kitchen, bathrooms, and closets in a wood-framed service wing that presents a low, almost windowless facade to the street and screens the taller, steel-framed stack of living areas, studio, and bedrooms behind. The distinction between these two volumes is also

The three-story rear facade with its expansive windows is screened by trees.

expressed in the stripes on the service wing. But this is also the south front, so Neumann broke out a glass bay to light the breakfast room and master bath below; the view from the kitchen is framed by a narrow horizontal slot.

To reduce the mass, the garage and foyer are pulled forward and linked to the house by a bridge with a peaked Kalwall [translucent fiberglass] vault that extends through the living area and is emphasized by an arrow-head deck leading out of the floor below. This axis is complemented by another that extends from a recessed east window to a diamond-shaped deck that projects from the west end. The top-floor living room is cut away to give added height to the family room and studio, creating a vertical flow of space that is emphasized by the diagonal wall that slices down behind the hearth.

"We achieved visual excitement at the price of quiet," says Neumann, who admits to a "compulsive desire to have the house look ordered and under control." But his elder son and daughter have grown and the second son is about to enter college, so that he and Beverly will soon have the house to themselves and their friends. The lower floor, housing the three children's bedrooms, can then be closed off from the rest of the house when it is not needed for guests.

The cool white volumes, flooded with soft, shadowless light, are enlivened by Beverly's exuberant art works and by the elegant furniture that Kenneth designed for the house. A tall shelf unit of mahogany, ebony, and bird's-eye maple with a knife-blade marble edge was inspired by a Paul Frankel "skyscraper" cabinet of the 1930s. The dining table has a glass top with sandblasted stripes, supported on columns modelled to suggest chess pawns. Shaker cabinets inspired the chest in the master bedroom, which has drawers of graduated depth and pulls that form an inverted V. "I thought I'd get to use half the drawers," says the architect, "but Beverly found she needed them all." ■

THIRD FLOOR

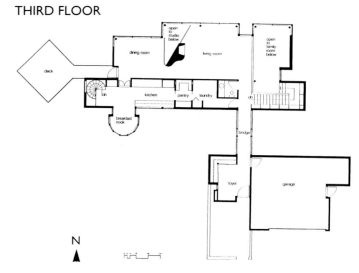

N
▲

SECOND FLOOR

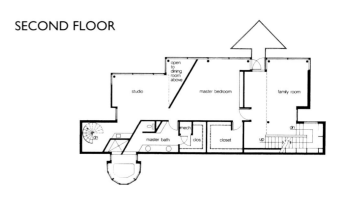

FIRST FLOOR

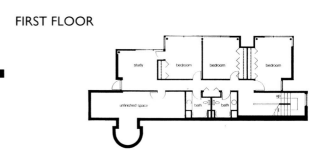

Opposite: Neumann's "skyscraper" cabinet was inspired by a Paul Frankel original.

An elegant abstraction of the colonial vernacular, hugging the slope below the road.

The upper living area is cut away to reveal the studio below.

MARK CIGOLLE (1949–) & KIM COLEMAN (1955–)

Santa Monica, California, 1987–92

MARK CIGOLLE worked for a quartet of A-list architects before opening his own office in New York, marrying and forming a partnership with Kim Coleman, and moving to Los Angeles, where they have designed a series of houses and large-scale projects. They extended an older house for themselves while deciding how they could live, raise a family, and work under one roof. Then they found a precipitous site that would baffle most builders but delighted them: a double lot, formerly a garden, on the east side of Santa Monica Canyon. It combined a view of hills and ocean, fresh air, and a feeling of the country close to the heart of the city.

"It's nice to design for yourself because you don't have to figure out what somebody else is thinking," says Mark. "Each of us got to wear three hats—designer, owner, and builder—and we kept switching roles. It was an opportunity to take risks and explore fresh ground." Adds Kim: "One of us would draw, the other would react. From the start, we saw the house as a set of parts, responding to the site, but we took time to consider different ways of doing it."

From these discussions and computer-assisted diagrams evolved a two-part, three-story, steel-frame structure: a rectilinear block aligned to the street and hugging the hillside, linked at each level to a 17-foot-square tower that is rotated outward to look down the canyon to the ocean. The separation is expressed in the materials: steel-trowelled gray stucco for the block, zinc-coated scales creating a diamond pattern on the tower. Wood, copper, and the red steel frame play off these silvery tones and heighten the ambiguity of openness and enclosure.

Like a crossword puzzle, the house can be read down or across. Vertically, it comprises work, living, and sleeping levels. The more intimate rooms—study, kitchen, and master bedroom—are stacked in the tower, and larger spaces—drafting office, living-entertaining, and a bed-playroom for their two small children—in the block, with the bridge areas as indoor-outdoor connectors. Steps lead

from the bottom floor down to the wedge-shaped garden and a covered play area beneath the tower.

The architects were their own contractors. They calculate that it cost 20 percent more to build on this slope, with its limited access and need for caissons, infill, and retaining walls. But they could never have built a 45-foot tower or enjoyed such spectacular vistas on a level plot. The steel frame allowed them to lighten the structure and open up the facades. As in the Neumann house, a low, reticent street front and double garage conceal the volume that steps down the hill, and the fragmentation makes it seem much smaller than its 6,500 square feet.

On the middle level, each room flows into the next, but has its own distinct character. The red steel staircase with its pale limestone treads seems to hover in the skylit hall, a sculpture that draws the eye and links the three levels. The living room captures the spirit of their New York loft: a muscular steel frame, exposed fir ceiling, maple-strip floor, overscaled seating, and zolotone cabinets in crisp black and white, with the California bonus of glass doors that slide back to open the room to the deck year-round. The dining room is screened from the den by a steel cross brace and a shimmering curtain. A curve of plywood encloses the stair that leads up to the tower study, a complement to the zinc scales and copper cladding on the other

UPPER LEVEL

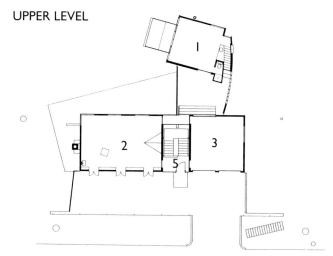

MIDDLE LEVEL

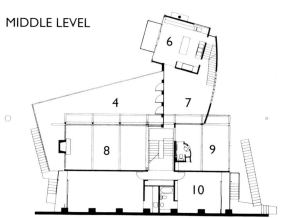

LOWER LEVEL

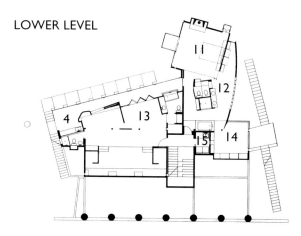

1. Study 2. Studio 3. Garage 4. Deck 5. Entry
6. Kitchen 7. Dining 8. Living 9. Den 10. Guest
Bedroom 11. Master Bedroom 12. Master Bath
13. Children's Bedroom 14. Closet 15. Laundry

Living room terrace and metal-clad tower.

walls. The children's room below has terraced play areas built into the hillside and a bright yellow wall that bows out below a clerestory to provide sleeping areas that can be enclosed when the children grow bigger.

"Our experiments were tempered by pragmatic issues," says Mark. "We wanted the house to have enduring quality and to be liveable—for ourselves and others—so that we shall be able to sell it and try again." It is hard to imagine a house that better exploits the potential of its site or achieves a more dramatic hierarchy of spaces, indoors and out. The five years that went into its making were well spent. ∎

Opposite: The red steel staircase with its limestone treads seems to hover in the skylit hall.

Overscaled monochromatic furniture complements the loft-like living room.

Zinc, copper, and steel play off plywood in the dining area.

Hollywood, California, 1989–93

TOURISTS SEARCHING for the Hollywood sign in a maze of hill roads often stop for directions at the foot of a new house that rivals the famous landmark in height and originality. The husband-wife partnership of Marc Angelil and Sarah Graham moved to Los Angeles from Boston and chose their "unbuildable" site on a sheer slope of Beachwood Canyon after considering the more conventional alternative of fixing up an old house in Venice. "We both love the ocean," says Sarah, "but, as Marc said, 'Why pay so much to live alongside hookers and tattoo artists?' Here we could build the foundations out of what we saved on the plot, use the house as a laboratory, and enjoy extraordinary views."

The couple divide their time between working and teaching in Los Angeles, and the practice that Marc established in his native Zurich. Current projects range from a new town center in Switzerland to a prototype lunch shelter for the Los Angeles school district. Each takes turns as project architect—"so that we don't kill each other," says Sarah—and she played that role on the house, though many of the ideas were developed between them.

Their competition entry for an extension to the American Library in Berlin inspired the concept of a precise T-beam structure, braced with tension cables at front and back, supporting a roof that floats over a rough wood box. The steel columns are supported on concrete beams, ten feet apart on center, which span three concrete retaining walls.

"Our goal was to express the elements, to let the structure speak," Sarah explains. "We took the model to a local engineer who wanted us to prop up the house and leave the tension cables as ornaments. 'Only you and I will know,' he said. So we went to Ove Arup [the firm that found a way to build the Sydney Opera House] and pleaded with them to help us. It was the smallest job they had ever done." The product of sophisticated engineering and unskilled labor is a 1,800-square-foot house that balances on the edge, figuratively and literally.

Mandatory setbacks on every side left only a narrow footprint on which to build, and their budget was equally tight. So Sarah and Marc expanded upward, creating a 20-foot-high living room and opening it up on three sides to garden

and deck through tall glass doors that slide, pivot, or roll up. Bedrooms and bathrooms are tucked away at the north end; a multi-purpose gallery is cantilevered over the kitchen and dining area at the center of the house. Walls are sheathed on the outside with industrial-grade plywood, which should bleach to gray; the roof is corrugated metal, and floors are surfaced with particle board. Cabinets and a two-story bookcase use construction-grade birch plywood. "The whole thing is an experiment, not our dream house," Sarah insists. "That's what allowed us to go forward. If you try to do things perfectly, you freeze."

Perfection was not in the contractor's vocabulary. The concrete for the retaining wall that flanks the lofty garage-studio was so badly poured that Marc had to

The house hugs an "unbuildable" slope in a canyon leading up to the Hollywood sign.

remember he was no longer in Zurich, where it would have been torn out and replaced. Later the couple were visiting one of their favorite buildings, Le Corbusier's monastery of La Tourette in

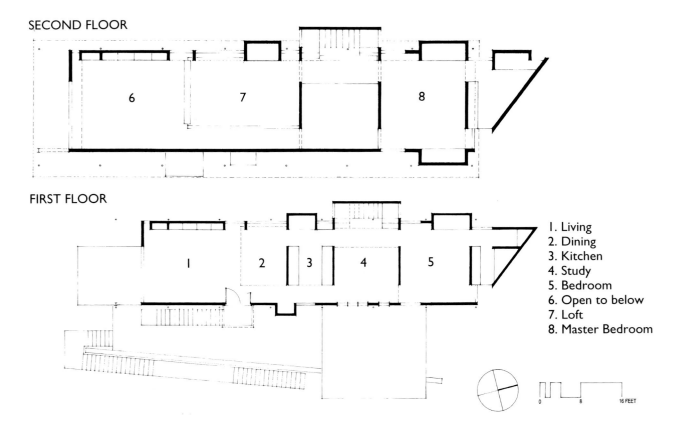

SECOND FLOOR

6

7

8

FIRST FLOOR

1

2 3 4 5

1. Living
2. Dining
3. Kitchen
4. Study
5. Bedroom
6. Open to below
7. Loft
8. Master Bedroom

0   8   16 FEET

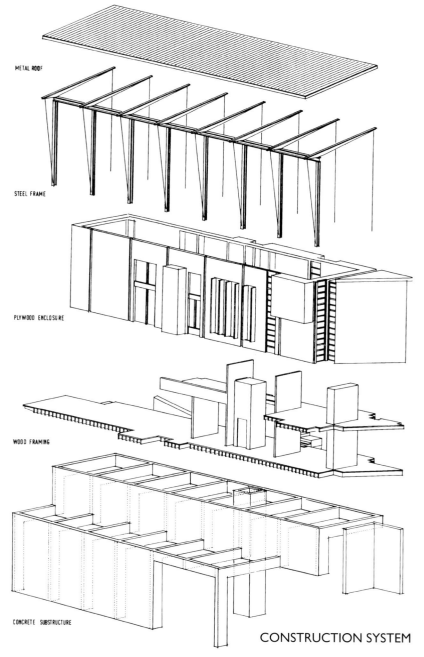

METAL ROOF

STEEL FRAME

PLYWOOD ENCLOSURE

WOOD FRAMING

CONCRETE SUBSTRUCTURE

CONSTRUCTION SYSTEM

France. Their Swiss friends were appalled by its coarse details and surfaces. "Marc and I were overjoyed to see, once again, that this magnificent architecture is able to accept rough craft," says Sarah. The offending wall in Hollywood will eventually be concealed by an expanse of red bougainvillea. Landscaping will soon obscure raw earth and structural supports, disguising the height of the house above the street.

The 10-foot module of the structure is plainly visible from within through a Plexiglas clerestory beneath the structural steel brackets. Windows draw your eyes up the slope and down to the street and offer fragmented views of hills and neighbors—including a battlemented castle with peacocks. The house is cooled by cross breezes and will be heated with the help of rooftop photovoltaic collectors. Raw wood, silvery steel, and white gypsum board conduct a dialogue of rough and smooth. It is a house that responds to its site and to the demanding tastes of its owners. "We took risks and enjoyed the process of building it," says Sarah. "We'd like to stay here for a while, but it would be fun to get another piece of land and try something new." ■

Opposite: A frame of steel T-beams, braced with tension cables, supports a roof that seems to float.

Overleaf: Looking through the double-height living room to the multi-purpose gallery. (© MICHAEL ARDEN)

New York City, 1976–79

REMEMBER THE MUSICALS Hollywood made to chase the Depression blues? Fred and Ginger dancing across a polished floor in a nightclub perched high above the glitter of New York? White on white decor, all created from plasterboard and mirrors on a sound stage? Imagine how a contemporary architect might realize that vision of urban sophistication, with steel, Plexiglas, and polished white plastic and marble, in a dizzying complex of spaces that seem to float above the real New York. Not that Paul Rudolph looks to Hollywood for inspiration—though if he had graduated in the Depression he might have headed west to design great movie sets. But his penthouse so dazzles the eye that you expect the band to strike up as you step through the door.

"Architects should build silly things they have an itch to do and wouldn't do for clients," says Rudolph. "I have had an apartment in this house on Beekman Place since 1962. I loved the light off the East River, but wanted to vary the ceiling heights. Human psychology demands a variety of spaces, so I built a three-story penthouse—to the consternation of my neighbors." He cantilevered the new structure six feet out from the facade, and Mrs. John D. Rockefeller, a near neighbor, made it known that she did not approve. Even Philip Johnson frowned. "I'm used to 40-feet cantilevers—this seemed more like a cornice," says Rudolph with an air of injured innocence.

"I didn't cross the building line. Everything on the street is different—I thought I was respecting that tradition."

Rudolph is no stranger to controversy. Students torched his Yale Arts and Architecture Building—a landmark of the 1960s—which they saw as the symbol of an oppressive establishment. Sober voices criticized its practicality, but few have denied the architect's mastery of light, mass, and volume, and the skill with which he weaves these together.

"I find it exhilarating to create for myself, but there is no sounding board," says Rudolph. "Vincent Scully, who is a friend, says I have too many ideas and that I don't know which are good and which bad." One indisputably good idea was to reinterpret the complex section of the Arts and Architecture Building, with its interlocking volumes and multiple levels, in lightweight, transparent materials. The monumentality of the Yale interior

MICHAEL WEBB

Right: Mezzanine dining and living room below—a dizzying complex of spaces.

The triplex perched atop a five-story, century-old house that overlooks the East River.

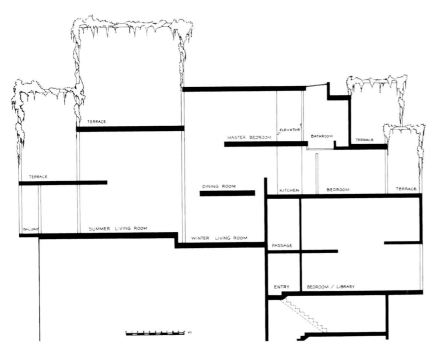

Labels in plan: TERRACE, TERRACE, TERRACE, BALCONY, SUMMER LIVING ROOM, MASTER BEDROOM, ELEVATOR, BATHROOM, TERRACE, DINING ROOM, KITCHEN, BEDROOM, TERRACE, WINTER LIVING ROOM, PASSAGE, ENTRY, BEDROOM / LIBRARY

is transformed into a three-dimensional labyrinth, shimmering in the light off the river. Escher might have drawn this complex of steps and voids, each leading onto the next, each mirrored and turned back on itself. These are not traps, but springs to send the spirits soaring—almost an anti-gravity machine.

The 3,600 square feet of enclosed space and 1,500 square feet of balconies and terraces are distributed on three and a half floors and 12 shifts of level. It's hard to be sure because Rudolph is constantly tinkering with the design. Low-ceilinged spaces—like the master bedroom—are cantilevered into voids. The architect enjoys the thought that he can sit in his Plexiglas Jacuzzi and look down through three levels. The Soane house—that

eccentric treasure, beloved by architects—inspired the openness that conducts light from clerestories and skylights to the core of the house, balancing the direct sun from east and west, and thus averting glare. Wisteria-hung pergolas project out at front and back, softening the jagged edges of the concrete walls and fostering a dialogue between this ethereal space and the solid brick buildings to either side.

There is an eclectic array of art works: a Picasso maquette of a kiss, Japanese robots, two transparent screens of Mexican votive offerings—tiny tin arms, legs, and hearts. Rudolph has even designed an invisible, mobile version of the classic Rietveld chair from slabs of Plexiglas mounted on casters. "All my life I've played with furniture and this is the only thing I have to show for it," he confesses. Every boy has his toys, and these provide diversion from his globe-trotting to far-flung commissions and stints in the office below. The triplex is open to water and sky, amenities most people have to leave the city to enjoy; it is serene but alert to the buzz of the city. ∎

Opposite: Library (below), dining area (center), and master bedroom (top).

New York City, 1989–90

IF PAUL RUDOLPH'S soaring, gleaming triplex may be compared to a big white set from a 1930s musical, Charles Gwathmey's apartment evokes Fred Astaire: impeccably stylish, every move precisely choreographed to look effortless, every hair in place; a shoo-in for Cole Porter's list of "tops." Rudolph's seems to dissolve in the reflected light off the river; Gwathmey's stands aloof, its windows framing the reservoir and towers across Central Park as though they were landscape paintings. It is a stone's throw from the Guggenheim Museum, which the firm of Gwathmey Siegel recently restored and expanded, provoking almost as heated a debate as did Rudolph's design for the Yale Arts and Architecture Building.

Gwathmey had lived on Fifth Avenue for years; when his children grew up, he bought a smaller apartment in the same building for the sake of its views. He gutted the interior and created a new structure within the shell. "I was interested to see if it could be dynamic and serene," he explains. "The constraints—of outer walls and ceilings, windows and elevators—were a stimulus to invention." In essence, he has fleshed out walls to give them depth and substance and dropped part of the ceiling to achieve a hierarchy of ceiling heights, from seven and a half to nine feet. Paradoxically, these encroachments and the harmony of proportions make the apartment feel even

more spacious than its 2,400 square feet, and suggest that a solid mass has been carved away. "I wanted to inflect the rectilinear space, laying one geometry over another, but keeping it incomplete," says Gwathmey. "Fragments are more interesting and mysterious than closed forms. It became a laboratory, with everything refined down to an eighth of an inch— and it drove my wife crazy."

The entry gallery widens, pulling you toward the natural light and drawing you into an ellipse that is defined by the hollowed wall, drop ceiling, and marble in the maple-strip floor. This subtle curve carries you around the corner, like the ovoid wall in Charles Moore's house, and reveals the grand climax: a living room that is perfectly aligned on a sculptured fireplace and on the three windowed fragments of Central Park. Delay enhances the gratification. Deep window reveals and four tones of white diffuse the light

through the room. Two rounded structural columns frame an intimate sitting area that Gwathmey has separated from the main space with a cabinet that is partly supported on an inverted cone—"my one and only experiment in deconstruction."

"I wanted to be surrounded by things I've collected over the years and to see if I could combine disparate objects harmoniously," says Gwathmey. This rigorous yet sensual apartment has an affinity to the refined interiors of the Vienna Secession around 1910, and contains chairs of springy elegance by Joseph Maria Olbrich and Josef Hoffman, plus a prototype Thonet chaise, alongside several modern classics. As a Fulbright scholar, traveling through Europe in 1962, Gwathmey made pilgrimages to the major buildings of Le Corbusier, and blew his savings on four Grand Confort steel-and-leather club chairs, which he still cherishes. The monochromatic palette of the room throws these pieces into sharp relief. Framed photographs are black and white; the only splash of strong color comes from a row of prints, Josef Albers's *Homage to the Square*.

Gwathmey has matched his artistry to that of his heroes, designing cherry and maple cabinetry that uses the leitmotif of a tiny square, notably in the master bed and radiator screens. His dining table takes its cues from the Hoffman chairs, with their shiny brass feet, and from a bevelled glass screen, also by Hoffman.

1. Elevator Lobby 2. Gallery 3. Closet 4. Bath
5. Bedroom 6. Service 7. Sitting Room 8. Living
9. Dining 10. Studio 11. Laundry 12. Mechanical
13. Kitchen

The twin bathrooms have onyx counters and sandblasted glass screens with polished centers that slide across the windows to provide backlit mirrors.

When this perfection palls, Gwathmey retreats to his tiny study where, surrounded by books, historic photos, and a tiny television to keep an eye on the ball game, he can plot more geometric adventures and remember the battles he has fought and won in the uncontrollable world beyond. ∎

Overleaf, left: An ellipse in the entrance gallery draws you into the apartment. (PAUL WARCHOL)

Overleaf, right: Living room windows frame views over the Central Park reservoir. (PAUL WARCHOL)

Dining area with chairs and a bevelled glass screen by Josef Hoffman beyond the sitting area.

Hoffman inspired the decorative motif of tiny squares in the master bedroom.

Seattle, Washington, 1986–87

JIM AND KATHERINE OLSON exchanged a 360-degree panorama of mountains and Puget Sound for a tightly focussed view of the city when they moved from a waterfront block to one in the heart of Old Town. "Friends thought we were crazy," says Olson, whose firm (Olson Sundberg) designed both blocks. "But here we can look out on the entire built history of the city, and it's a fascinating neighborhood, with music wafting up at all hours from jazz clubs and street musicians." It also provided a fresh start. As he explains: "I've always thought of my own apartments as places to experiment with unproven ideas before I try them out on our clients."

Among those clients are several of Seattle's leading art patrons, and Olson himself is a passionate collector and contemporary art activist. "I had always wanted to be an artist and instead became an architect," he admits. So it is no surprise that his duplex is full of site-specific art works and is itself an installation that manipulates scale, perspective, and light inventively.

The eighth-floor entry takes you into a skylit shaft that rises 30 feet through both levels of the apartment. A prism catches the sun and casts a shifting rainbow streak across the walls, drawing your eyes upward. Olson calls it "an urban sanctuary that takes you out of the world before you step back into the real world. In the future, people are going to have to live in tighter quarters," he continues. "If we can give them psychological space, we don't have to provide as much physical room. The Japanese have long understood how to frame small spaces to make them go further—indoors and in their gardens."

His goal was to exploit his 1,400-square-foot interior to the limit, but without making it feel cramped. Living, dining, and bedrooms all open onto terraces through sliding glass doors. The living room floor is like a tray, turned up at the sides, and its 11-foot ceiling is masked by a suspended, backlit cove, so that the side walls appear to flow past without touching, like the shaft of an open-cage elevator, and you feel you could be miles up in space. Jeffrey Bishop painted the dark-blue, red-accented murals with their Lascaux-like figures mingling with cosmic images; Nancy Mee's totems of stacked glass give this other-worldly vision added depth. The colors pick up on the red and gray facade of the Romanesque-style Pioneer Building

MICHAEL WEBB

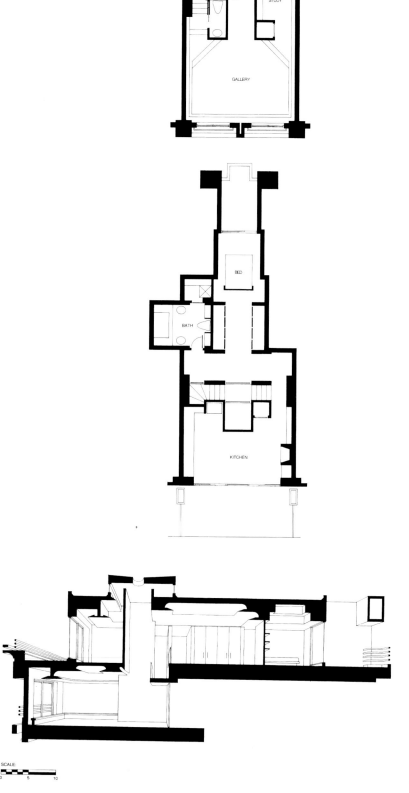

across the street, which, framed by expansive windows, becomes the fourth, detached wall of the room.

As a native of the Northwest, Olson understands how to exploit the region's misty gray light, warming it with earthy tones. Pale gray and shades of white dematerialize the inner walls, like the mists that often veil the downtown high-rises and set off the rich hues of polished wood, leather, and oriental rugs. Floors and stairs are surfaced with inexpensive, hard-wearing chipboard that is finished to resemble granite. This, however, was a bright notion that the architect may spare his clients. Each board had to be sponged, sprayed with airplane wing sealant, and perfectly fitted into place. It would have been cheaper to have used the real thing. Little strips of copper bring a sparkle to the stair treads, and glass balustrades reflect the light.

Narrow steps lead up to the dining room-kitchen and to a bridge that over-looks the living room and provides refuge for a dense concentration of objects that seem, like driftwood, to have settled into every nook. The bedroom is just large enough to contain the bed, but it is warmed by the soft, rose-brown tone of the walls and expanded by the stepped-up ceiling and view out over old roofs, waterfront cranes, and a partial view of Puget Sound. The lack of elbow room

Opposite: Jeffrey Bishop's mural seems to flow past the floor and ceiling of the living area.

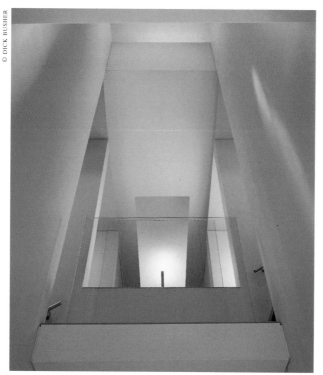

seems not to bother the Olsons. Insists Katherine: "This is such a comfortable room, especially when our two dogs are sleeping in the drawer that pulls out from the foot of the bed, and everyone is breathing together." Jim jokes that whenever he gets tired of this world he can levitate in his sleep, like a dead Pharaoh, into the tomb-like void above the bed. ∎

Sun striking a prism casts a rainbow on the shaft that rises through both levels of the apartment.

The Pioneer Building in Seattle's Old Town becomes a fourth wall to the living room.

STEVEN MENSCH (1943–)

New York City, 1989–91

STEVEN MENSCH has built a steel, glass, and brick temple, flanked by trees, that's as handsomely proportioned and finished as Philip Johnson's Glass House. The principal difference is that it's located 20 feet above ground within the shell of a brick warehouse in New York's West Village. And Mensch doesn't live in it. The temple is a courtyard, with a retractable glass roof and walls, that brings light and air to a compact two-story apartment at one end and a lofty painting studio at the other. After spending the week here, working in monastic seclusion, he returns to his wife, children, and dogs in their pre-Revolutionary Pennsylvania farmhouse.

Mensch was trained as an architect, joined the faculty at Cornell after getting his master's, and started his own design and construction company in Ithaca. "I switched from architecture to painting in order to keep my sanity," he says. "I hated having to begin the morning by yelling at contractors. I was frustrated by waiting on others and seeing my work changed. With art, I'm in control." He found a loft in New York City, where a friend showed him a warehouse that had been built in 1890 as a carriage barn, and later chopped down from five stories to two. He bought it for its unusual width and raw space and reshaped it over three years of design and construction.

The once-handsome Romanesque facade was mostly gone, and it would have been cheaper to tear it down, but the neighborhood enjoyed landmark protection. Nor could he afford to restore it: there were nine different kinds of brick, none of which could be easily replaced. So he decided to strip later additions, clean it, and leave the fragment as a free-standing ruin, with a new brick enclosure set a few feet back—a strategy that won him a city preservation award. Inside, he kept the six-bay structural frame and columns of the ground-floor space, and leased it out.

"I've built for myself before, but this was the first time I had the money and opportunity to do it right," says Mensch. "When I'm in the city I work all the time and hardly go out, so I wanted a contemplative space, with lots of light and air. For me, the greatest luxury is a big empty room." He struggled with the proportions, designing his studio as a 19-foot cube within a canopy that is supported by two

MICHAEL WEBB

slender columns. The living space is minimal, with a few chairs and a table, a narrow wedge of a kitchen in which to make coffee, and an upstairs sleeping gallery. A narrow flight of brick steps lead up from the entrance past two mezzanine-level guest bedrooms he provided for his eldest sons. The greatest challenge was to fit a precise building into an irregular shell.

The building department insisted on as much open-air space as if this had been a 20-story tower. Eventually, it compromised on an all-weather, 19 x 38-foot atrium. "Press a button, everything slides back and you are out of doors," says the proud owner. "Often I just sit here and look at it; the purity of geometry and the intensity are inspiring." Bronze frogs spout water into a shallow pool. Sunlight is filtered through the leaves of the zelkova trees planted along narrow mezzanine terraces and down through the glass-brick pool base to the rental space below. In summer, the courtyard catches the breezes and provides a romantic setting for occasional dinner parties. In winter, the glass roof is a passive solar collector, but Mensch enjoys the sensation of rain splashing on his doorstep, and opens the roof as often as he can. And in every season, it expands the living spaces and adds a pastoral flavor to city living.

Inside, everything is polished perfection, from the heated, black granite floors to the meticulously welded black steel frame. Like Kroeger, but in a radically different way, Mensch has stripped away the inessential to focus singlemindedly on his large, exuberant canvases. And when he has done, the messy vitality of the city is close at hand; a balcony looks out on a real-life version of Hitchcock's *Rear Window* set. ■

"Ruined" facade conceals a new studio apartment in New York's West Village.

Longitudinal section through the new structure.

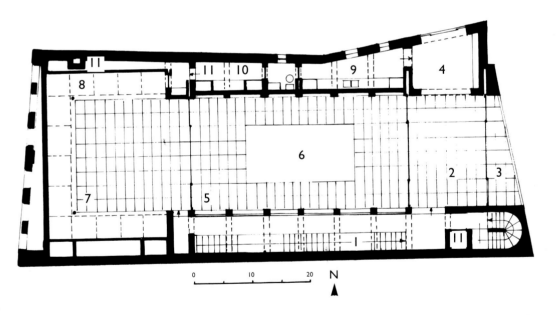

0   10   20   N
▲

1. Stair up from entrance 2. Living 3. Balcony 4. Dining 5. Court 6. Pond/Skylight 7. Studio 8. Skylight above
9. Kitchen 10. Bath 11. Storage

***Overleaf: Rooms look inward to a steel and glass
atrium that opens to the sky.*** (© MICHAEL MUNDY)

193

Looking from the bedroom to the painting studio at the far end of the atrium.

The living room is polished and stripped to essentials.

JOSEPH GIOVANNINI (1945–)

New York City, 1989–93

"WHENEVER I'm in a room I have a strong urge to redesign it," says Joseph Giovannini, who first succumbed to the impulse in Rome, remodelling two small apartments in a palace on the Via Giulia, while studying at the School of Fine Arts. Since then he has become a passionate advocate of deconstructivism, drawing on his background in French philosophy, his love of baroque illusionism, and the daring proposals of the Russian avant-garde in the 1920s. But his mastery of arcane theory has not contaminated his writing, nor lessened his sense of adventure in turning theory into practice—notably in his transformation of the midtown New York apartment he shares with his wife, Christine Pittel, who also writes on architecture and design.

He bought it as a fixer-upper in 1985, 800 square feet of boxy rooms in a handsome art deco tower. Previous remodelings—of a loft in Montreal and a tiny Manhattan studio—had given him the experience of sculpting space hands-on, using his eye rather than construction drawings. A major conversion in nearby Gramercy Park became a showcase of eccentric angles and layered planes. "Subversive ideas can be injected into

1. Living
2. Study
3. Kitchen
4. Hall
5. Bedroom
6. Bath

Overleaf: View from the living room into the study and the kitchen on left. (© JUDITH TURNER)

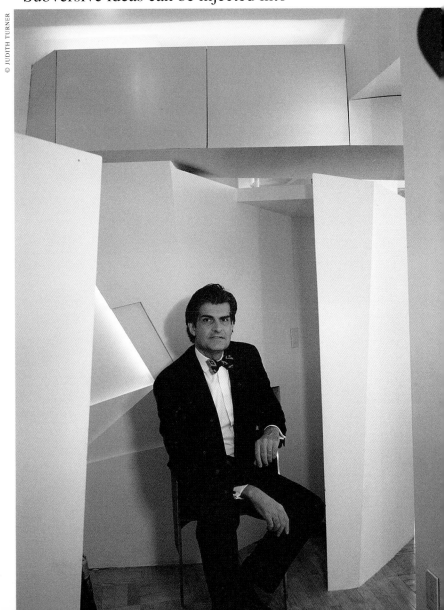

© JUDITH TURNER

any situation," he insists. "Even in Grosse Pointe I was able to turn a colonial revival house into something delirious." In his own apartment he tore out existing room divisions and purchased a built-in closet from a neighbor (only in New York!) to extend his boundary line. Then he began plotting how to articulate the space and to create a bedroom, study, and open living-dining area within a volume only a Japanese would consider spacious. (It's worth remarking that Giovannini is 6-foot-5 and that his wife is an enthusiastic collector.)

"In my own apartment I cannot not go the limit," he declares. "But it all comes down to a couple of ideas and three materials. [The first idea is the struggle for territory.] Rooms grab space from other rooms and defend themselves—like the competition of cars and people at the intersection of 57th Street and Lexington Avenue. The plan is a map of the battle. The second idea was to work with a moving vanishing point, shifting away from classical Renaissance perspective, in which all lines converge at a fixed point on the horizon. I was inspired by Kandinsky, Malevich, and Al Held. Artists are the advanced guard for architecture."

A ship's carpenter interpreted the complex drawings, crafting flying planes, jutting beams, and tilted enclosures from a wood frame clad in materials that shimmer in the light: bleached anigré wood, Kemcore (a silvered laminate), and white sheetrock. The goal is to dematerialize the space and defy gravity; to provide places to sit, sleep, work, and eat, but to distract the eye from the mechanics. Bookcases and closets are constructed in forced perspective. We are accustomed to seeing this in John Okulich's wall reliefs and the drawings of the Russian Constructivists, but it is only now being realized full-scale in three dimensions. An inlay of deep green marble traces the outline of the old apartment, a tangible memory of what was removed.

"I think of this project as the eye speaking to the mind," explains the architect. One of his heroes is Guarino Guarini, who created domes of dazzling ingenuity in late baroque churches in Turin. But it is easier to admire a work of art, high above or on a wall, than to live in one. Artists have often created idiosyncratic environments that had little appeal to anyone else. Giovannini remarks that he could go further in his own apartment because he didn't have to ask a client's permission, but his geometric experiment is firmly rooted in the interiors he has created for others. It stretches the envelope a little further, testing concepts that may be developed on a larger scale elsewhere. But it should be judged not just as a demonstration of theory, but as an inventive way of energizing a small space and making it more habitable. ■

Sheffield, Massachusetts, 1975–

"OUR FIRST IDEA," recalls Hugh Hardy, "was a trailer and a porch on my family's land in the Berkshires, a place we could take the kids on summer weekends from New York. Instead, we built a skinny rectangular wood box, with exposed studs, a shed roof with a fiberglass skylight, and a sleeping tower. The simplest possible shelter—I designed it in my head driving up here." It grew bigger with his two children and, though they have now left home, Hardy continues to add—a pool house, a laundry and second tool shed—to please himself and his wife, Tiziana. There are enough towers to suggest a rustic San Gimignano. "With the right box of building blocks you can play indefinitely," he jokes.

Hugh and Tiziana Hardy beside their acroterion.

HHPA

Fresh out of Princeton, Hardy went to work with his hero, stage designer Jo Mielziner, and then with Eero Saarinen on the Vivian Beaumont Theater, before establishing his architectural practice in New York. He was soon joined by Malcolm Holzman and Norman Pfeiffer, and their partnership made its reputation on creative adaptations of old structures and new buildings that used more dash than cash. Theaters—from the Majestic in Brooklyn to the Alaska Center for the Performing Arts—have been their specialty. So it is no surprise to see how inventively Hardy manipulates a few simple elements to create a presence on the 26-acre site and a welcoming interior. "The goal was to get the most for the least," he says. "If I wanted to be fancy I would use shiplap boards and shingles; this shows how you can make do with cheap materials."

The shed roofs and towers suggest Victorian forms, leaving the mind to fill in the blanks. The square towers are set at a 45-degree angle to the rectangular rooms. "I colored it gray to make it fade away," says Hardy. "I didn't want it to look conspicuous, because it's the landscape that's important. Everything is one room thick and positioned to look out in different directions." From the screen doors and decks flow axes aligned on outbuildings and landscape features—like the carved stone acroterion (stylized leaf) that the architect acquired from the roof

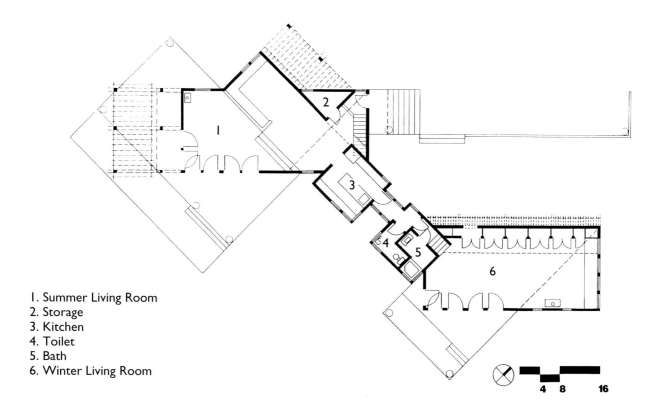

1. Summer Living Room
2. Storage
3. Kitchen
4. Toilet
5. Bath
6. Winter Living Room

4 8   16

The shed roofs and towers suggest Victorian forms. (MICHAEL WEBB)

Looking from the garden sheds back to the house.

of a vintage Wall Street skyscraper during demolition.

The addition was a duplicate of the first house in plan, but with a gallery-study, reached by a secret stair. It is also better insulated. "We discovered that first summer how cold it can get in August," says Tiziana. Old-fashioned iron stoves allow the house to be used almost year-round. The space flows easily, from the original living room, through the improved kitchen to the new dining room (a total of 2,000 square feet). Color and stencilled patterns enliven the bleached fir boards. When they were small, Sebastian slept on a triangular platform overlooking the living room; Penelope enjoyed what her parents call "the princess suite," with its crystal chandelier, lace curtains, and painted frieze of P's. Now they've grown and left these rooms for guests. The parents, disdaining convention, still sleep up a narrow flight of stairs and bathe in a closet; higher up is an observation turret, reached by a ladder. The pool house, with its sleeping gallery, guest rooms, and comfortable living area, is a miniature of the main house.

"Serious contemporary architects, like Philip Johnson," says Hardy in a mock serious tone, "make their additions in the latest style; mine are all of a piece. But it's all scenery, and you have to paint it every year." ■

Dining room and gallery in the addition.

Original living room, now used only in summer.

Lakeside, Michigan, 1982–87

A 90-MINUTE DRIVE from Chicago around the south rim of Lake Michigan brings you to a village that was, in turn, a lumber-shipping port, a fashionable resort, and an artists' colony. It then went into a long decline but is now being rediscovered. Stanley Tigerman and Margaret McCurry built their weekend cottage where the Armors and Swifts once summered. They had searched for something old but could not find a place they liked, so this odd couple collaborated on a fusion of new and old.

Tigerman is an erudite enfant terrible with an eclectic practice, who believes in "architecture couched in humor, architecture that is fun." A native Chicagoan, he lives in a Mies apartment close to his office, had never before owned a house, and refused to drive more than 90 minutes from the city. McCurry designed interiors for Skidmore, Owings & Merrill, began her own practice, then married and became partners with Tigerman. She has Irish roots and is a passionate gardener.

They wanted the house to be a family gathering place—both have children from previous marriages—but small and inexpensive. McCurry calculated the spaces they would need, working from the inside out, on a footprint of 800 square feet—the minimum that local regulations would allow. "Stanley would have made everything too small," she says. Each had a different vision. "She saw it as a Shaker meeting house; I thought of it as a piazza with rooms leading off," says Tigerman. "I drew most of it, and had the power of the pencil, but she contributed more to the overall design. If she disagreed with what I had proposed, she would tell the contractor what she wanted—there were no working drawings."

The product of disagreements, improvisation, and off-the-shelf materials is a little jewel. The 20 x 40-foot house has a pitched tin roof, side walls of corrugated, galvanized steel that step in to suggest a loft rising from a shed, and flat end walls of gray-painted marine plywood faced

MICHAEL WEBB

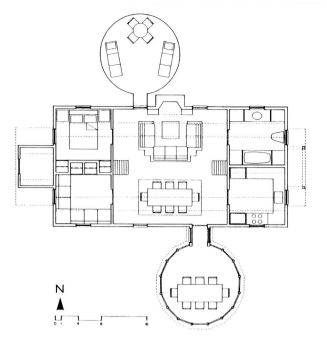

N
▲
0 1   4   8   16

A wooden walkway links entry, house, and gazebo.

The house and porch were inspired by local farm buildings, and by Italian basilicas and baptisteries.

in white lattice. Attached is a circular screen porch, capped with a conical silo roof. Together they evoke traditional barns and granaries and suggest to the architects—who had just returned from Rome—a primitive basilica and baptistery. "We search for an authentic American architecture, and find hybrids," says Tigerman. Locals took the rustic association more literally: barns are for animals, not people. They assumed this was a city slicker's fantasy or a joke at their expense, and passed an ordinance forbidding the use of corrugated metal on houses.

Over the next five years, the architects added a raised wood walkway that curves out like a baroque colonnade to link an entry gate to the house and continues its half circle across a pond to a screened gazebo and pump house. A porch-like garden shed was attached to the front of

Opposite: Storage lofts double as sleeping galleries.
(JIM HEDRICH / © HEDRICH-BLESSING)

Central living area, enlivened by folk art, soars to the full height of the vault.

the house, and, to extend the axis over the water, a model Tuscan temple of corrugated metal sits in the pond. The farm has been transformed into a pleasure pavilion, elegant and allusive despite its humble materials, reaching toward objects in the landscape.

All of McCurry's skills were deployed in the lofty interior. A tiny bathroom, kitchen, and two bedrooms occupy the corners beneath a sleeping gallery at either end. To secure a permit, these were dubbed storage lofts, since they can be reached only by steps, with no handrail, that are as steep and narrow as a ladder. Galleries and the upper side walls squeeze the central living space, but the axial symmetry counters this compression. The windows are small, to assure privacy and a sense of enclosure. "We are outdoors all summer," explains McCurry, "and we have picture windows in our Chicago apartment." French windows open to the garden, fans turn lazily overhead, and folk art enlivens the cool palette. The cross-braced screen porch serves as an airy dining room and as shelter from summer showers.

"We built this for ourselves, with no intention of luring or impressing clients," says Tigerman. However, it works as well for a house party as for a busy couple seeking solitude, and other professionals are following their lead. On a clear day you can glimpse the tops of Chicago's towers, 50 miles across the water, but this house seems to belong to a different world and era. ∎

The Monument, Joshua Tree, California, 1987–90

TWO HOURS' DRIVE FROM LOS ANGELES, in a lunar landscape of granite rocks, there appears a clustered trio of red, blue, and green blocks, seemingly dropped here by a playful giant. A local, riding by, reins in his horse to gaze at this apparition. "That a house? People goin' to live there?" he asks. Told they are, he shakes his head. "Must be architecture," he remarks as he rides away.

Josh Schweitzer (with colleagues at Schweitzer BIM) designed this 950-square-foot house as a place where he and his wife, Mary Sue Milliken, a top Los Angeles chef, could weekend with friends in the high desert. He had won acclaim for several restaurants located in old buildings, and later did an exemplary remodel of Diane Keaton's 1928 Lloyd Wright house in Hollywood. But this was his first ground-up project, and he jokingly dubbed it "The Monument." He spent days at the 10-acre site, located just

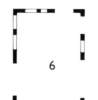

1. Living
2. Dining
3. Kitchen (Loft over)
4. Bath (Loft over)
5. Bedroom
6. Gazebo

outside the Joshua Tree National Monument, striving to express the spirit of place and to integrate the house with the giant rocks—and thinking how different it was from the prairies of Kansas where he was raised.

His goal was to amplify and abstract what he found on the site, and to create a sense of order amid chaos. A first design—comprising linked bedrooms with tilted walls, a detached pyramid-shaped living room, and a monumental arch—sent local builders into shock. Schweitzer went back to his drafting

Overleaf: A clustered trio of brightly colored blocks, seemingly dropped by a playful giant. (© TOM BONNER)

table. "I wanted to go beyond the right angle, but realized I had to do something straight up and down if I wanted to get it built," he says. Ironically, when it was done the straight walls were three inches out of alignment. To please himself, he subverted the rectilinearity of the plan with a series of what he calls "wacky windows." And he created a dynamic relationship between the blocks: a free-standing gazebo and pavilions for living and sleeping that are linked by a tiny kitchen. He wanted to suggest that the surrounding rocks had been sliced and reassembled to create simple boxes, with openings that evoked the crevices between them.

Each block took its color from nature. "Everyone thinks of the desert as mono-chromatic, and tries to blend in," says Schweitzer. "But when you look careful-ly, there are all these amazing colors: a vivid green lichen growing on a rock, a bright red flower and the impossibly blue sky. This compound takes those colors and employs them at the scale of man, which is bigger than the flowers, but a lot smaller than the rocks."

The linked pavilions provide a cool refuge from the heat of summer. Tones of lime, ocher, mustard, and brick animate the interiors and help absorb the sun's glare. The south wall is solid, but light streams in from six glass doors and win-dows that seem to have been carved from the walls with a sharp knife. They frame expressive fragments of rock and distant mountains, contrasting with the wide-screen spectacle you enjoy when you step outside. Each wall is a satisfying diagram of sharp angles that complements its neighbors and becomes part of a layered composition of vistas and reflections, solids and voids. Sleeping lofts cut into the 18-foot-high rooms. You feel protect-ed and enclosed, but always connected. The spirit of the desert flows through, like wind from an open door.

As the sun sets behind the mountains, the colors in and on the house seem to intensify before fading to black. Concealed lighting gives the interiors a soft glow. Candles on a table transform the gazebo into a huge jack o' lantern, the golden light streaming out into the dark-ness through sharply cut eyes and teeth. The French philosopher Blaise Pascal wrote of the terror he felt in contemplat-ing the universe, with its eternal silence and infinite space. This house captures the immensity and silence of the desert and gives resonance to the laughter of friends. ■

Opposite, top: The gazebo serves as a shady retreat from the fierce desert sun.

Bottom: Bright colors were inspired by wildflowers, the angled windows by rock fissures.

ULRICH FRANZEN (1922–)

Bridgehampton, New York, 1978–79

AN UNREPENTANT MODERNIST, Ulrich Franzen is happy to admit that "the most important influence in my life was Mies," but his own work has a gentle, humane quality that is well exemplified in the 61 residences he has designed, including this weekend cottage. In the 1980s the Hamptons became as much a symbol of vulgar excess as Newport, Rhode Island, had been in an earlier era. Overscaled beach houses, each shouting for attention, rose side-by-side along the dunes. Franzen had his choice of sites, and characteristically he chose the inland side of the coast road, facing north over a saline pond. "It is full of wildlife and much more restful than the ocean," he remarks, and the wisdom of his choice was validated by a major storm that devastated his neighbors on the beach.

"I wanted to work with the horizontal lines of the site," he says, "but to make a sharp distinction between the natural and the man-made. At the time it seemed like an imposition on the land; now I wish I had included more space so that I could spend longer out here. It's smaller than my apartment in the city." The house floats 10 feet over a sea of bayberry bushes, on a platform of girders supported by heavy wooden piles designed to protect it from hurricane flooding. Its white-stained cedar siding, rounded corner, porthole openings, glass brick, and pipe railing on the stairs and roof deck all evoke a 1937 streamline moderne beach pavilion. You half expect to see blazers, straw boaters and print frocks, and to hear Gershwin on the Victrola.

It is a year-round house, with decks for every season. A rakish gangway leads up from a stepped wood jetty, and you board the good ship Franzen across a kind of quarter deck that serves as an outdoor foyer. The circular opening in the screen wall resembles a moon gate and serves, like its Chinese antecedents, to compose the view—over the wetlands to the old cottages that emphasize the flatness of the land. Steps lead up to the roof deck.

The house that looked so modest from the street feels more like its 1,900 (enclosed) square feet when you step through the door and take in the sweep of the horizontal and vertical planes, extending out to the horizon through a ribbon of windows. There is a feeling of release, which the architect intended. "I wanted to hold back a sense of discovery," he says, "not every room should have a view." A curved wall separates the kitchen-dining area from the small living room and the

MICHAEL WEBB

A streamline moderne beach pavilion floating over a sea of bayberry bushes.

covered deck beyond. Three bedrooms along the south side screen these rooms from the street. Steps and a walkway lead down to a fourth deck that seems to be moored, like a dinghy, beside the pond.

The house has no need of air conditioning because ocean breezes sweep through unimpeded. Color dramatizes these simple volumes: intense orange and maroon at the center of the house, subtle gradations of beige, white, and muted hues around the perimeter. "We used 14 different colors and drove the painters crazy," Franzen recalls. "We proceeded by trial and error, and many of the surfaces had to be repainted."

"Openness and light were the goals, and a simplicity that looks even better today," he says. "Back then, white was considered very old-fashioned." Time has approved his taste, and the Society for the

Preservation of Long Island Antiquities has given the house its stamp of approval. But Franzen has no thought of resting here. His dream is to build a house that grows from the ground atop a mesa in New Mexico. "I haven't found the site or the money yet," he says, "but I will." ∎

1. Dining/Kitchen
2. Living
3. Master Bedroom
4. Guest Bedrooms

A circular opening in the wall of the outdoor foyer frames the wetlands beyond.

Planes extend to the horizon through a ribbon of windows which command sweeping views.

Subtle colors and simple furnishings make the living room a peaceful escape from the city.

Jasper, Georgia, 1990–91

TERRY SARGENT spends his week designing schools and research laboratories as a partner in one of Atlanta's larger firms and his weekends in a mountain cabin he named for his wife, Jean Wineman, a professor of architecture at Georgia Tech. They were fortunate to find a development, an hour north of the city, where every plot has been sold but few have been built on. Squirrels, mockingbirds, deer, and racoons are their only neighbors on the thickly forested site, which drops steeply down from the road to a lake.

Sargent designed a tall skinny wood-framed house (16 x 72 feet), running north-south to follow the contours and minimize excavation of the underlying rock. He was able to preserve all the big pine trees, which shade the expansive east and west windows in summer but allow for solar gain in winter. The thin section and full glazing provide dramatic views up and down the slope from almost every room in the house. Cross ventilation is boosted by ceiling fans. This rational, energy-efficient design was almost rejected by the local review board, which thought it looked like a mobile home and feared the owner would divide it in two and sublease. Even now, locals call it "the trailer house."

In this remote location, Sargent chose the simplest form of construction—a balloon frame of 4 x 4s, sheathed in local pine, with a protective base and retaining walls clad in local stone. "Everything in the house came from the quarry, lumber yard, or hardware store," he says proudly, "and we bought all the furniture in one trip to the Pine Factory." His contractor urged him to cover up some of the pine-walled interior with gypsum board to make the house easier to sell, but he stood firm. For the exterior he used the vernacular "moody bevel," a thick clapboard that, properly sealed, provides good protection from sun and snow.

"As an architect who grew up under the influence of the Bauhaus, I had to have a modular grid," admits Sargent. The 2 x 8-foot module was right for the walls and windows, but I insisted on using it for the stairs as well—the builder thought I was crazy. It is perverse, but I like the tightness. Usually it's a miserable experience dealing with uneven workmanship, but here I decided to let go and accept the roughness." He had no complaints about the local masons, who created the "dry stack" chimney and double-sided hearths on both floors.

Terry Sargent, Jean Wineman, and their children.

TERRANCE SARGENT

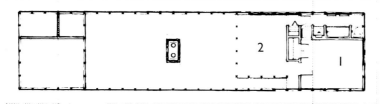

UPPER LEVEL

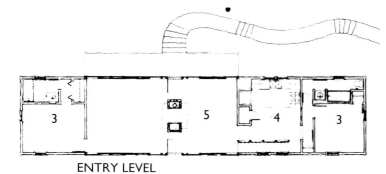

ENTRY LEVEL

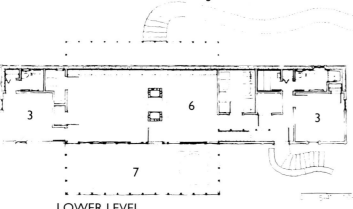

LOWER LEVEL

1. Master Bedroom 2. Study 3. Bedrooms 4. Kitchen
5. Living 6. Playroom 7. Screen Porch

A mountain cabin designed with a thin section to maximize views and natural ventilation.

The house was sited to preserve the largest pines.

Local masons built the "dry-stack" chimney that rises through the lofty interior.

The product of his calculations, of local craft and carpentry is a rigorous rusticity, perfectly matched to the site and the family's needs. The interior combines drama, intimacy, and practicality. The pitched roof over the parents' bedroom and open study gives the feeling of being in a tiny cabin, floating above the lofty living area. The roof cascades down and flips up—like the flourish at the end of a signature—over a guest bedroom at the south end. Rooms for their three daughters are tucked in below the parents' and guest rooms, with a playroom opening onto a screen porch below the living area.

The architect permitted himself one more flourish midway through construction. The septic tank had been incorrectly sited, below the projecting screen porch. To sidestep the tank and support the porch, he designed a pair of branched wood brackets, similar to those that Alvar Aalto used in the vault of a library in Finland. It demonstrates in miniature the ingenuity and wit that Sargent brings to multi-million-dollar projects. But, he says, "When I come here, I leave the problems of the city behind and concentrate on drawing, which is what I enjoy most." ∎

ADAM KALKIN (1962–)

Gay Head, Martha's Vineyard, Massachusetts, 1989–90

AWAY FROM THE MANICURED STREETS of Edgartown, the bustle of the ferry port, and the Methodists' whimsical campground at Oak Bluffs, Martha's Vineyard has a bleak beauty that makes every house appear to be an act of defiance against nature. Saltboxes, old and new, stand tall in the expanses of windblown brush. Other buildings huddle together for mutual protection from winter gales. The tourist season is brief; only the toughest live here year-round.

Adam Kalkin, a versatile designer, seized by what he calls "the brutal energy you have when you've just finished school," built a house that captures the raw spirit of the island. It is hidden from the road, which makes the discovery of this impressive debut all the more exciting. Boxy black and metallic volumes collide and interpenetrate, touch a rock outcrop at one corner, and are lofted above a gentle descending slope on concrete posts and telegraph poles. Steps lead up to other entrances, and steel poles support decks that command sweeping views of land and ocean. Part sculpture, part industrial shed, the structure has a rude poetry that may not please majority taste, but which is surely preferable to the ersatz gentility of most new construction in this area.

Kalkin had been going to the Vineyard for years with his parents and decided to establish his own foothold there when he returned from the Architectural Association School in London. "It was the first project I had built," he says. "At first I was going to build a simple cottage, and then I thought—why not do something different? My interest in architecture is finding out about things I don't know."

His sense of adventure was spurred by a newspaper ad offering two buildings for sale at a bargain price: a Vermont barn, turned diner, and a steel warehouse in North Dakota. He bought them both, had them disassembled and shipped to the site, and then began figuring out what he could do with his pile of "blocks." "Each was expressive of a different technology and era," Kalkin notes. "What interested me was the relationship between them." Working hands-on for a year with Stephen DeLong and a few other friends, he interwove the two, exploiting the soaring, wood-framed volume of the barn, and the plain, rectilinear space of the workshop to create an integrated whole. Punching in through a corner of the workshop at second-floor level is a wing

The disassembled parts of a barn and a warehouse were shipped to the site and fused together.

of guest bedrooms, clad in tar-coated plywood.

The 3,000-square-foot interior offers the same mix of collision and collage and a flexible shelter for owner and guests. The spacious living room is contained within the volume of the barn, and the master bedroom is above it; the brightly lit kitchen-dining area is in the projecting workshop. This creates a division between "old" and "new" similar to that in Frank Gehry's remodelled house. Here, too, is a layering of space, from light to dark and up through the metal gratings that serve as a floor for the mezzanine: provocative juxtapositions of sharp and soft and a play of sunlight and reflections. But this weekend house is rougher and

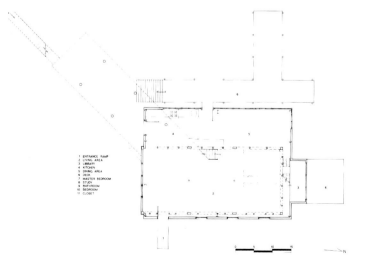

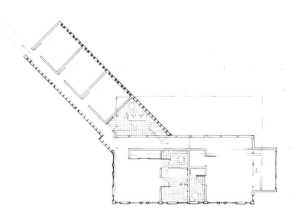

more improvised than Gehry's; it is a habitable sculpture infused with the "brutal energy" Kalkin brought to it.

Another, more whimsical side of his talent is revealed in his Soho loft. The master bed is mounted on stilts and curtained; a guest bed is enclosed in a closet on wheels, with a spy hole that reveals an antique painting behind; a stair with fold-up treads leads to an office above.

The vacation house has a new owner—proof that experiments can be sold—and Kalkin is tackling larger projects, collaborating with other artists on the design of exhibitions, and dreaming of fresh adventures. ■

Intersecting beams at the center of the house.

Part sculpture, part industrial shed, the house commands sweeping views but is invisible from the road.

MARC ANGELIL and SARAH GRAHAM
(Angelil/Graham, Architecture Urban Planning Interior Design,
6105 Melrose Avenue, Los Angeles, CA 90038; 213 871 1450)

MARK CIGOLLE and KIM COLEMAN
(Cigolle/Coleman Architecture,
455 Upper Mesa Road, Santa Monica, CA 90402; 310 454 3684)
James Steele. *Los Angeles Architecture* (London: Phaidon Press/
Chronicle Books, 1993)

ROBERT D. DRIPPS and LUCIA PHINNEY
(Architecture & Urbanism,
PO Box 60, Route 692, Batesville, VA 22924; 804 823 4969)

CHARLES and RAY EAMES
(house in Pacific Palisades, CA; no tours)
Blueprints for Modern Living: History and Legacy of the Case Study Houses
(Cambridge: MIT Press, 1989).
John and Marilyn Neuhart, Ray Eames. *Eames Design* (New York:
Harry N. Abrams, 1989)

RICHARD FERNAU (Fernau & Hartman, Architects,
2512 Ninth Street, #2, Berkeley, CA 94710; 510 848 4480)
Sally Woodbridge. *Bay Area Houses* (Layton, UT: Gibbs Smith, 1988).
Progressive Architecture (August 1991)

ULRICH FRANZEN FAIA
(Ulrich Franzen & Associates, Architects & Planners,
168 E 74th Street, New York, NY 10021; 212 535 3631)
Architectural Record Houses (April 1979)

ALBERT FREY
(686 Palisades Drive, Palm Springs, CA 92262; 619 325 2851)
Joseph Rosa. *Albert Frey, Architect* (New York: Rizzoli International,
1990)

FRANK O. GEHRY FAIA (Frank O. Gehry & Associates,
1520B Cloverfield Blvd, Santa Monica, CA 90404; 310 828 6088)
Architecture of Frank Gehry (Walker Art Center. Distributed by Rizzoli
International, 1987)

JOSEPH GIOVANNINI
(140 E 40th Street, New York, NY 10016; 212 297 0980)
Joseph Giovannini. *On Deconstruction* (New York: Knopf, 1994)

MYRON GOLDFINGER FAIA
(584 Broadway, New York, NY 10012; 212 966 5007)
Myron Goldfinger (New York: Artium Books, 1992).
Myron Goldfinger. *Villages in the Sun* (New York: Rizzoli International,
1967/1993)

WALTER GROPIUS
(house at 68 Baker Bridge Road, Lincoln, MA.
Tours. June 1- October 15: Fr, Sa & Su noon-4PM; November-May:
first full weekend of each month, noon-4PM. Information & group
reservations: Society for the Preservation of New England Antiquities,
141 Cambridge St, Boston, MA 02114; 617 227 3956)
Reginald Isaacs. *Gropius: an Illustrated Biography of the Creator of the
Bauhaus* (Boston: Bullfinch Press, 1991).
Nancy Curtis. *Gropius House* (Boston: SPNEA, 1988)

CHARLES GWATHMEY FAIA
(Gwathmey Siegel & Associates, Architects,
475 Tenth Avenue, New York, NY 10018; 212 947 1240)
Gwathmey Siegel: *Buildings & Projects 1984-92* (New York: Rizzoli
International, 1993)

HUGH HARDY FAIA (Hardy Holzman Pfeiffer Associates,
902 Broadway, New York, NY 10010; 212 677 6030)
Hardy Holzman Pfeiffer (New York: Rizzoli International, 1992)

DAVID C. HOVEY (Optima Inc,
630 Vernon Avenue, Glencoe, IL 60022; 708 835 8400)

CARLOS JIMENEZ (Architectural Design Studio,
1116 Willard Street, Houston, TX 77006; 713 520 7248)
Carlos Jimenez (Barcelona: Gustavo Gili. Distributed by Rizzoli
International, 1991)

PHILIP JOHNSON FAIA (Philip Johnson Architects,
885 Third Avenue, New York, NY 10022; 212 230 2112)
David Whitney and Jeffrey Kipnis, eds. *Philip Johnson: The Glass House*
(New York: Pantheon Press, 1993).
Architectural Digest (Vincent Scully review; November 1986)

ADAM KALKIN (Kalkin & Co,
900 Mt Kemble Avenue, Morristown, NJ 07960; 201 425 1918)
Progressive Architecture (July 1990)

RAYMOND KAPPE FAIA (Kappe Architects Planners,
715 Brooktree Road, Pacific Palisades, CA 90272; 310 459 7791)
Toshio Jutaku (Tokyo, March 1982)

TIMOTHY KOBE and JOY OU (Kobeou Associates,
675 California Street, San Francisco, CA 94108; 415 394 6090)
James Shay and Christopher Irion. *New Architecture San Francisco*
(San Francisco: Chronicle Books, 1991)

HANK KONING and JULIE EIZENBERG
(Koning-Eizenberg Architecture,
1550 18th Street, Santa Monica, CA 90404; 310 208 6131)

KEITH R. KROEGER (Kroeger Woods Associates, Architects,
255 King Street, Chappaqua, NY 10514; 914 238 5381)
Jill Herbers. *Great Adaptations* (New York: Whitney Library of Design,
1990)

DONALD McKAY (Donald McKay & Co,
515 Queen Street W, #200, Toronto, Canada M5V 2B4;
416 594 6800)
Canadian Architect (January 1993)

RONEY J. MATEU
(Harper Carreno Mateu, Architecture Engineering Interior Design,
4217 Ponce de Leon Blvd, Coral Gables, FL 33146; 305 441 0888
Maurice Culot and Jean-Francois Lejeune. *Miami: Architecture of the
Tropics* (New York: Princeton Architectural Press, 1993)

STEVEN MENSCH
(727 Washington Street, New York, NY 10014; 212 645 7410)

CHARLES W. MOORE FAIA (Moore/Andersson Architects, 2102 Quarry Road, Austin, TX 78703; 512 476 5780)
Eugene Johnson, ed. *Charles Moore: Buildings & Projects 1949-86* (New York: Rizzoli International, 1986).
Charles Moore, Gerald Allen & Donlyn Lyndon. *The Place of Houses* (New York: Henry Holt, 1979)

WALTER A. NETSCH FAIA
(1700 N Hudson Avenue, Chicago, IL 60614; 312 944 7924)
Inland Architect (Chicago, May-June 1990)

KENNETH NEUMANN FAIA (Kenneth Neumann/Joel Smith & Associates, Architecture Planning Interior Design, 400 Galleria Officentre, Southfield, MI 48034; 313 352 8310)
Inland Architect (Chicago, May 1985)

RICHARD NEUTRA
(VDL house at 1900 Silverlake Blvd, Los Angeles, CA 90039)
Open by appointment: Public Affairs Coordinator, College of Environmental Design, California State Polytechnic University, 714 869 2664)
Thomas S. Hines. *Richard Neutra and the Search for Modern Design* (New York: Oxford University Press, 1982).
The Richard and Dion Neutra VDL Research House I and II (California State Polytechnic University, Pomona, 1985)

HERBERT S. NEWMAN FAIA (Herbert S. Newman & Partners, Architecture Planning Interior Design, 300 York Street, New Haven, CT 06511; 203 772 1990)
Architectural Record Houses (April 1985)

JIM OLSON FAIA (Olson Sundberg Architects, 108 First Avenue S, 4th fl, Seattle, WA 98104; 206 624 5670)

ALFRED BROWNING PARKER
(RD 3, Box 1530, Bristol, VT 05443; 802 453 4245)
A. B. Parker. *You and Architecture* (New York: Delacorte Press, 1965)

BART PRINCE
(3501 Monte Vista NE, Albuquerque, NM 87106; 505 256 1961)
Christopher Mead. *Space for the Continuous Present in the Residential Architecture of Bart Prince* (Albuquerque: University of New Mexico Art Museum, 1989)

JEFFERSON B. RILEY FAIA
(Centerbrook Architects, Box 995, Essex, CT 06426; 203 767 0175)
Michael J. Crosbie. *Centerbrook: Reinventing American Architecture* (Washington DC: AIA Press, 1993)

PAUL M. RUDOLPH FAIA (Paul Rudolph Architect, 23 Beekman Place, New York, NY 10022; 212 752 7365)
World Architecture 19 (September 1992).

TERRANCE E. SARGENT (Lord Aeck Sargent, Architecture, 1201 Peachtree Street NE, 400 Colony Square, #300, Atlanta, GA 30361; 404 872 0330)

R. M. SCHINDLER
(house at 835 N Kings Road, West Hollywood, CA 90069. Open Sa-Su, 1-4pm, and by appointment, 213 651 1510)
Lionel March and Judith Sheine, eds. *R.M. Schindler: Composition and Construction* (London: Academy Editions, 1993).
Kathryn Smith. *Schindler House, 1921-22* (Los Angeles: Friends of the Schindler House, 1987)

WARREN R. SCHWARTZ (Schwartz/Silver Architects, 530 Atlantic Avenue, Boston, MA 02210; 617 542 6650)
Architectural Record Houses (April 1987)

JOSH SCHWEITZER (Schweitzer BIM, 6406 Homewood Avenue, Hollywood, CA 90028; 213 962 5530)

MARK SIMON (Centerbrook Architects, Box 995, Essex, CT 06426; 203 767 0175)

LAURINDA SPEAR FAIA and BERNARDO FORT-BRESCIA FAIA
(Arquitectonica International, 2151 LeJeune Road, #300, Coral Gables, FL 33134; 305 442 9381)
Beth Dunlop. *Arquitectonica* (Washington DC: AIA Press, 1991)

LAWRENCE W. SPECK
(8 Cromwell Hill, Austin, TX 78703; 512 471 5111)
Landmarks of Texas Architecture (Austin: UT Press, 1986)

WILLIAM F. STERN (William F. Stern & Associates, Architects, 4902 Travis Street, Houston, TX 77002; 713 527 0186)
Architectural Review (London, July 1992)

STANLEY TIGERMAN FAIA and MARGARET I. McCURRY FAIA
(Tigerman McCurry Architects, 444 N Wells Street, Chicago, IL 60610; 312 644 5880)
Stanley Tigerman: Buildings & Projects 1966-89 (New York: Rizzoli International, 1989).
Architectural Digest (Vincent Scully review; April 1984)

RAQUEL VERT
(18039 Karen Drive, Encino, CA 91316; 818 708 1177)

BERNARD M. WHARTON (Shope Reno Wharton Associates, Architecture & Interior Architecture, 18 W Putnam Avenue, Greenwich, CT 06830; 203 869 7250)

FRANK LLOYD WRIGHT
(house at Taliesin West, 13201 N 108th Street at Cactus Rd, Scottsdale, AZ 85261; 602 860 2700. Tours daily: October-May, 10am-4pm; June-September, 8-11am)
Terence Riley, ed. *Frank Lloyd Wright—Architect* (New York: Museum of Modern Art, 1994).
Frank Lloyd Wright Selected Houses 3: Taliesin West (Tokyo: Global Architecture, 1989)

BUZZ YUDELL (Moore Ruble Yudell, Architects & Planners, 933 Pico Blvd, Santa Monica, CA 90405; 310 450 1400)
James Steele. *Moore Ruble Yudell* (London: Academy Editions, 1992)

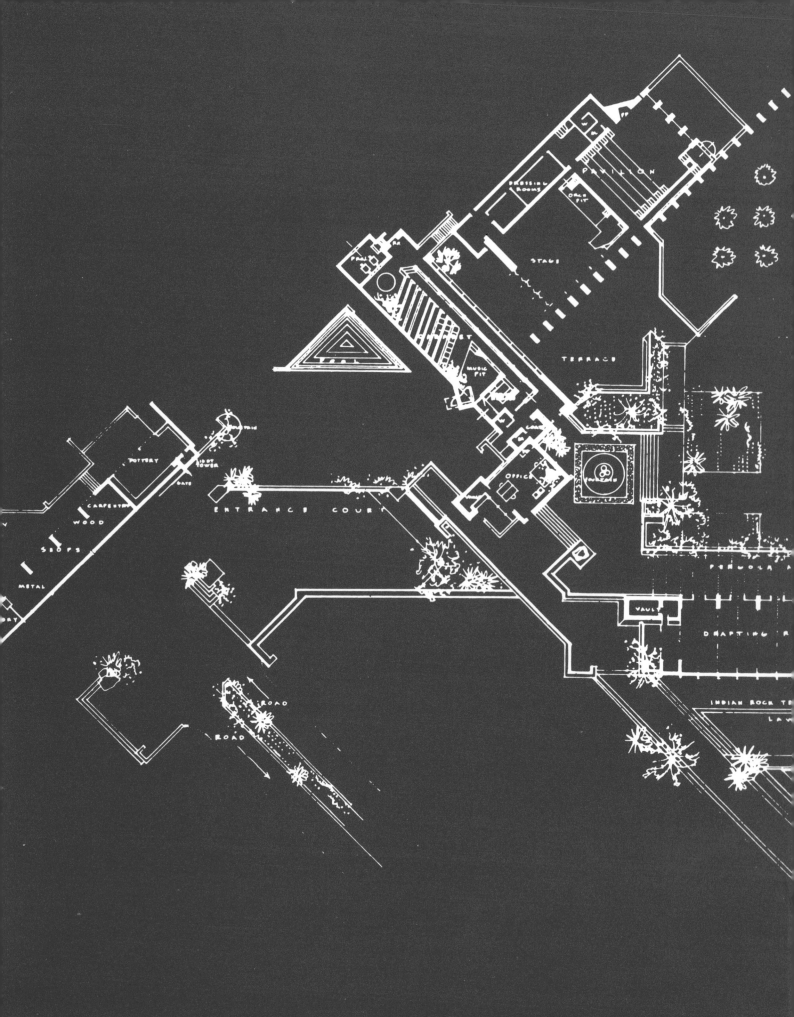